A WAKEFUL FAITH

A WAKEFUL FAITH

Spiritual Practice in the Real World

J. Marshall Jenkins

UPPER
ROOM BOOKS™
NASHVILLE

Cover design: Gore Studio, Inc.
Cover photograph: © Index Stock Imagery
First Printing: 2000

Library of Congress Cataloging-in-Publication Data

Jenkins, J. Marshall, 1957-
    A wakeful faith: spiritual practice in the real world / J. Marshall Jenkins.
      p.   cm.
    Includes bibliographical references (p.).
    ISBN 0-8358-0912-9
    1. Christian life.   I. Title.
  BV4501.2.J434 2000
  248.4—dc21   99-32602
                                                  CIP

Printed in the United States of America.

For my devoted parents,
Rees and Betty Jenkins;
my loving wife, Sharon,
and our precious son, Philip

Through all of you,
God has blessed me each day of my life.

CONTENTS

PREFACE

Each day brings a flood of demands for our time and attention. The pot boils over. The power bill comes due. The dog throws up. With a full appointment book, no time remains for a report due tomorrow. I have eight new e-mail messages to read as the regular mail stacks up. The television ads say I really should consider flood insurance and another breakfast cereal. I cut short quality time with my family for a phone call. Then I go to bed feeling guilty.

Day by day we cope by selective inattention and forgetting. Some do not return calls. Others do not listen to their co-workers' concerns or their spouse's needs. We find ways to divert ourselves with TV, food, overwork, or hobbies. Those who seek to include religion amidst the madness often pursue it as an escape, ever careful to filter out its demands for their time and attention. After all, we call the place of worship a sanctuary.

So we put religion into a compartment and allot it a fair share of our time and energy. We vary from person to person on how much time and energy we grant it, but most of us keep it in its place. We may worship and pray and sing with utmost sincerity and spirit on Sunday mornings. Yet, in the rough and tumble of returning phone calls, chewing out or getting chewed out at work, and washing endless laundry, we block it out. Meanwhile, some of us hope that God mercifully attends to us despite our inattention. Others feel guilty enough and hope that God has better things to do than to watch us elbow our way through this daily madness.

Deep down, many of us feel that the pace is killing us, but we do not admit it very often. After all, everyone else seems to get along okay. Something is killing us, but it is not the pace. It is the inattention to our deepest desire, the desire for God.

It runs contrary to common sense, but Jesus called us to seek first the kingdom of God. In other words, God reigns over all things, so we cannot escape. We profit more by facing the reality of God in our daily lives. Jesus calls us to live in awareness of God's reign over our whole lives, not just a part. As demanding as that sounds, Jesus promised that such commitment will not overburden us. It will set us free.

Free from what? Not free from stress or suffering or even uncertainty. Rather, living awake to God in all our daily affairs sets us free from meaninglessness. The hectic pace and excessive demands of our lives sap our sense of vocation as Christians, the meaning and purpose of our lives. The better question is not, "Free from what?" but "Free to what?" Watchfulness for Christ in our midst sets us free to lose our lives that we may find life in his kingdom today, not just at the end of history or after physical death.

The chapters that follow will offer reflections on some of Jesus' teachings about the kingdom, especially those in which he calls us to be awake and to watch. Additional reflections on biblical passages and themes that shed light on the wakeful life will appear. Examination of various dimensions of daily life will make use of these biblical reflections as we seek a deeper understanding of the wakeful life in Christ.

At the outset, I wish to acknowledge a few limitations. I cannot catalogue every dimension and detail of daily life important to everyone, and this book either omits or mentions only in passing numerous aspects of daily life. Surely most readers will finish the book with a critique that begins with the phrase, "I wish he had said something about . . ." While I hope to have adequately focused on the greater part of the daily lives of most readers, please forgive me for those parts dear to you that I omit. Think of reading this book as a conversation with a spiritual friend. Take what you can use to enrich your perspective, and use this book as a stimulus to develop your own approach to wakefulness in areas not addressed or inadequately addressed here. Perhaps someday I will have the good fortune of learning from you.

Since I wrote the book to stimulate prayer, personal reflection, and group conversation, I minimized the use of quotations and references to supplementary sources. Endnotes appear where I used quotations or explicitly discussed the contents of other books, but I used them sparingly in order to keep the flow of the book at a conversational level. I wrote as a pilgrim addressing other pilgrims, not as a scholar imparting new knowledge.

I focused on biblical material that I find personally helpful in forming the wakefulness of my faith, limited as I am. While I seek to allow the scripture to speak for itself, oversimplification of the Bible's messages occurs all too easily in supplementary material like this book. If the critical reader detects neglect or questionable interpretation of relevant biblical material, please forgive me the inadvertent but inevitable flaw. Understand that my journey in biblical understanding and wakeful faith is far from over. Seize the opportunity to enrich your perspective through reflection and prayer on the problem, and pray that God will guide us both.

Given the personal, conversational nature of the text, my personality, socioeconomic status, gender, race, and stage along the way of faith limits the book's scope. Again, think of reading this book as a conversation with a spiritual friend. My prayer is that God will lead the reader to insights beyond those that my personal limitations will allow at this time.

This book will be useful for both individual and group study. I wrote it to address the concerns of individuals ranging from pastors to lay leaders to seekers considering the assimilation of the Christian faith into all aspects of their lives. Moreover, I consider the integration of our spirituality into our daily life an urgent need for the church. Thus, I hope study groups in the church will use the book. Each chapter ends with three questions for reflection and discussion that will enable individuals to carry their thoughts further than the text allows and that will stimulate group discussion and intimacy.

Finally, I eagerly acknowledge those who have supported me spiritually, emotionally, and intellectually in ways that made this book possible. Sharon, my wife, shares my days and nights with me, prays with me, and patiently critiques my writing. She brings many blessings to my daily life, and I cannot imagine this book or anything else of value in my life without her part in it. I am also continually grateful for the constant love of my parents and family (in-laws included). Such love gives us strength for long hauls like writing books.

Roger Martin, recently retired, has served as more than my pastor. He is my spiritual guide who takes an hour each month to hear me ramble about my walk with God. He certainly deserves credit for bits of clarity that show through in this text from time to time.

Finally, the small communities in which I live make this book possible. As Director of Counseling at Berry College, I work with a wonderfully supportive Vice-President for Student Affairs and a first rate staff. Moreover, I serve students whose courage and honesty continually inspire me. Similarly, clients in my private practice enrich my life by sharing their struggles, their doubts, and their faith with me. Those who worship and study the Bible with me at our church also help me keep my eyes open to God's work in the church and the world. All of these people make it easier for me to discuss my everyday world as an arena through which God addresses me lovingly.

PART I

The Way of Wakefulness

CHAPTER 1

Lessons from Squirrels, Citizens, and Saints

WHY WE GET UP IN THE MORNING

My alarm clock sounds, a shrill bleating that snatches me abruptly out of deep sleep like a fish on the line. I see the fluorescent red digits, 6:00, and I see them still after I turn off the alarm and look away, the afterimage sweeping the darkness with my gaze. As the afterimage fades, the day's first decision comes to the fore: Shall I get up now?

I do so without asking why. My getting up implies faith that the question, "Why should I get up?" has an answer, although I am too groggy to conjure it up. Yet, sooner or later, I will ask it.

"Why do I get up in the morning?" is an expression for, "What is the meaning of my life?" If I do anything at all today, I must do it for some purpose beyond myself that contributes meaning to my life. Otherwise, I might as well stay in bed and count the tiles on the ceiling.

Most of us will never fully know why we get up in the morning, at least not in this lifetime. However, many of us will know that a reliable Guide leads us on

an adventurous journey toward a meaningful destination. We call that knowledge faith. How clearly
we obtain it depends on how awake we become after
the alarm sounds. This chapter discusses the differ-
ences between ordinary wakefulness and the higher
wakefulness that finds meaning in life, and it intro-
duces Jesus as one who challenges us to reach that
higher wakefulness.

THREE LEVELS OF WAKEFULNESS

There are three levels of wakefulness.

At the first level of surface wakefulness, we
resemble squirrels, vigilant for danger and food and
shelter. The squirrel keeps a watch constantly while
gathering and feeding on acorns in the grass. Every
movement within eyeshot evokes a quiver or jerk,
the tiny body curling and dashing, curling and dashing. The hair on its tail stands up constantly in an
airy plume that jerks and recoils with every real and
imagined threat. The beady eyes open wide and
black, ever alarmed.

Quick and agile if a dog rushes toward it, the
squirrel adapts well, responds well to a world of
monsters and acorns. The proficient squirrel knows
escape routes and how to use them. It stores up extra
acorns if it feels a harsh winter coming in the wind
or in the tremors of the ground.

Most of us live in the squirrel's wakefulness most
of the time. At our best, we vigilantly seek and
respond to threats near or far. We adapt well, taking
care of ourselves and our own. It's not necessarily a
bad life at this level: We save our money, buy a
house, take care of our children, find ways to enjoy

life without stepping on too many toes.

But everything we do concerns survival, so we can make no sense of death.

Some of us move on to a second level of wakefulness. We want to talk back to death, to find an answer to it. Adaptation and survival shrink in this awareness, and we develop a hazy notion that it makes sense to lose one's life in order to find it. We still do not know what that means, but we trust that it means something. This is the beginning of faith.

Like the squirrel, we still hold fast to feeling the wind and gauging the planet's trembling. We cannot control the wind or the earth's crust. So we watch the expressions in the eyes of others, and when we do, we find that our eyes have an impact. We cannot control their eyes, but somehow when the others' eyes meet ours, they darken or dance or spark. We move from the squirrel level to the citizen level, aware of our life in a community, faces transmitting signs of life from one to the other like electricity.

When we move from the squirrel level to the citizen level, we change. We become more concerned with what we give than with what we have. We want to help the younger generation grow and the older one smell the roses. Meanwhile, we seek real closeness and honesty with family and friends. Social justice, community care, and intimacy replace adaptation and competition in our list of priorities.

We try to deal with death by truly looking into each other's eyes now while we live. When I die, maybe the memory of my eyes will make another's eyes dance and darken and twinkle. Maybe when I decay, another will grow, nurtured in part by the memory of me.

This is the noble wakefulness of citizenship. This wakefulness draws us into community. Yet, we cross the threshold of death alone, and this wakefulness cannot bear the loneliness of death.

The third and deepest level of wakefulness teaches us something more from looking into the others' eyes. At this level, the influence of my eyes on the others' eyes no longer captivates me. The uncontrollable mystery does. The invisibility of the wind moves me more than the feel of it. The stillness of the earth frightens me more than its trembling.

At this level, the wakefulness of the saints, every set of eyes that I encounter seems a shadowy reflection of other eyes, God's eyes. God becomes the Other whom I long to know. Yet, mystery shrouds this Other. I develop an inviting and terrible sense that I am known. This becomes all the more terrible when I find that I cannot see the eyes of the knowing Other.

Perhaps in time I find that I could not bear seeing those eyes. "No one shall see me and live," God said to Moses on the mountaintop when Moses' longing to see God got the best of him. Perhaps the Other mercifully chooses to hide.

This leaves me subject to the invisible wind. It leaves me with both feet on the ground. It enables me to embrace mystery. And once I learn to embrace mystery and wait for the gaze of the Other, I am prepared to die.

LIVING IN SURVIVAL MODE

Psychologist Abraham Maslow proposed that we humans possess a hierarchy of needs. At the lowest level, basic needs such as food and shelter involve survival. Moving up the ladder, more social needs such as love and power motivate us. Atop the hierarchy, if we ever get there by taking care of all the needs below it, we strive to meet a need for self-actualization, the full realization of our potential, the dynamic expression in our work and values and relationships of our truest selves.[1]

This theory challenges us to grow beyond survival needs. It challenges psychologists and everyone else to move themselves and others to higher levels of growth and consciousness. It challenges us to direct our energies toward more intimate relationships and creative self-expression rather than bogging ourselves down with anxious scurrying to pay the light bill or make a killing in the stock market. The economic boom after World War II, the development of airplanes and microwaves and home computers, and the geometric proliferation of knowledge at universities all bolstered our faith in human progress, including personal growth. Maslow's theory gives us stair steps that rise with our optimistic upward gaze.

Yet, thanks to Charles Darwin, we know better. Darwin preceded Maslow, and Darwin reminded us how much we have in common with squirrels. He put them in our family tree (no pun intended). We evolved from them or with them and shared the same basic needs, and both species live by survival of the fittest. Thus, survival sets the standard of all that we do, everything to which we aspire, how well we escape danger, how well we gather for the winter.[2]

Maslow showed us the stairway to self-actualization, but Darwin had already nailed the door shut. While their views are not theoretically incompatible, historical experience strongly suggests that the struggle for survival plays a more dominant role in human nature than the self's drive to reach its potential. Greed, war, persecution, petty partisanship, social indifference, and other sorry states remain historical constants, miring us in mediocrity. Since Maslow refused to look beyond human nature for answers, dust gathers on the idea of self-actualization as a realistic aspiration.

This notion that we live primarily in survival mode may sound odd. After all, we Americans live in the wealthiest, most technologically advanced nation ever. Surely with the drudgery of the kitchen removed by microwaves and dishwashers, the toils of laundry reduced by washers and dryers, and the exchange of information speeded by word processors and the Internet, we should have time for our loved ones and our souls. At least that was what the salespeople said who convinced us to buy all those gadgets in the first place.

Yet, the idea that we live primarily in survival mode probably comes as no shock to the single mother working two jobs to feed the kids and pay the bills with nothing left over to replace her runny stockings. It still will not shock her after she earns that college degree and moves up to a management job that seems to demand more time and energy than the two jobs she held before the kids became moody teenagers. The insurance company vice-president with the mid-life crisis and the shredded conscience from an extramarital affair realizes all too painfully that his dreams never got far beyond the survival level.

Despite modest profits of late, the chain-smoking company president contemplates more downsizing to avoid the nightmare of bankruptcy if the pendulum ever swings too far the other way. That is survival mode at its saddest, when the fear of losing wealth drives the wealthy. Considering the increasing concentration of money among the rich while the single mothers working two jobs get less real dollars for their heroic efforts, one suspects that the fear of losing wealth remains all too common at the top.

As we enter the twenty-first century, the struggle for survival still sets the agenda, not the soaring flight to self-actualization. We conquered space, sending men to the moon and traveling about the globe in a frenzy scarcely imagined one hundred years ago. We will never fully overcome time—we all must die—but we made inroads, practically doubling our life expectancies through the wonders of modern medicine. These achievements required enormous ingenuity and will power and hard work.

But moving beyond survival mode requires something more than the pioneering, inventive, and aggressive spirit that got us here. It requires awe, a "fear of the LORD" as the Old Testament writers called it. It requires humility and relinquishment, an admission of weakness that finds power in God. Divine foolishness is wiser than our wisdom, divine weakness stronger than our strength, wrote Paul (1 Corinthians 1:25). We must succumb to mystery after so many years of explaining mystery away.

Few cross over into the twenty-first century without a pang of disappointment. The crowning achievements of science and technology seem to be bombs—atomic bombs, truck bombs, mail bombs. Our leaders have violated our trust and broken promises many times, and the media, knowing the thirst of the wounded and suspicious for bad news about others, sells papers and news shows through a flood of cynical reporting.

Children beget children and shoot out the windows of homes or shoot their classmates and teachers just to act out a part they saw on the late movie. In our fear and confusion, we go out and buy a gun. Entire communities of once hopeful and patriotic Americans have become so fearful and confused that they amass arsenals to defend themselves against "the government"—a catchword for those faceless outsiders who supposedly caused their fear and confusion.

These observations may seem tiresome and redundant, like another read of the afternoon paper. We've heard it all before, that we are poor in spite of our wealth, fearful in spite of our comforts, that the struggle to survive goes on. What the newspaper will not tell us is that Jesus came, not to offer sentimental moral adages or a heavenly escape route. He came to pray with us, "Thy kingdom come, Thy will be done, on earth as it is in heaven"—on earth with all its bombs and hungers and anxieties, as in heaven. And he is still here, wooing us and cajoling us, declaring that we can live in the kingdom here and now if we will get out of survival mode and awaken.

THE PROMISE OF THE KINGDOM

"Jesus came to Galilee, proclaiming the good news of God, and saying, 'The time is fulfilled, and the kingdom of God has come near; repent, and believe in the good news'" (Mark 1:14-15). Thus, Jesus began his teaching of the kingdom of God, the central theme of his whole life and ministry. When we think of the chaos and disarray of our earthly kingdoms discussed above, we welcome the promise of another kingdom, a new order.

Jesus' listeners on the dusty roads and windy shores of Galilee certainly welcomed his teaching of the kingdom with that hope. The Romans occupied their nation and taxed them so heavily that they could not get ahead. Their destiny rested in the hands of heavily armed aliens who understood neither their faith nor their love for the land.

Jesus' disciples hoped for a new kingdom under God. To this day we find in Jesus' teachings the hope that someday God will intervene and dry our tears and calm our fears and keep us safely. That remains a crucial part of the promise of God's reign on this earth.

Yet, that part of the promise can also blind us because our half-awake ideas of the kingdom confuse much of Jesus' meaning. No sooner had Jesus praised Peter for being the first to openly identify Jesus as the Messiah, than Jesus had to rebuke Peter for understanding his lordship in terms of worldly fame and power (Matthew 16:13-28). Perhaps Judas Iscariot betrayed Jesus after losing patience with him for not marshaling the political resistance to Rome that his popularity and healing power seemed to make possible.

We cannot help making the same mistakes because we are at best half-awake most of the time. We impose our economic, political, and personal expectations on the kingdom, so we miss out on the kingdom at hand. If we like the word *progressive*, we imagine a kingdom in which people embrace change and eagerly pursue every enhancement of life that science and technology can provide. If we like the word *conservative*, we imagine a kingdom of the self-made, accumulating the wealth and goods for which we dream and taking responsibility for it without interference from others. If we like the word *liberal*, we imagine a kingdom of cooperation in which everyone takes care of each other, takes from each according to their abilities and gives to each according to their needs. Yet, the closer we read Jesus' teachings, the more he shakes our expectations and forces us to pay attention to the kingdom that is here, now.

That raises another aspect of Jesus' teaching that we easily miss. True, he spoke of a kingdom in the future, but he also spoke of it in the present. When Jesus announced the theme of his ministry in the quotation from Mark cited earlier, he did not say the kingdom of God *will* come; rather, he said, "The kingdom of God *has come near*" (emphasis mine). Only awakening to the kingdom of God in our midst now will prepare us for the coming kingdom.

That is our paradoxical plight: the kingdom is here and the kingdom is not yet. We struggle to survive. Thus, the kingdom is yet to come. Surely we must get up in the morning to prepare for it.

Yet, Jesus conquered death and lives with us amid the struggle itself. Surely we must get up in the morning to praise him for it. We must awaken. Through the higher wakefulness that Jesus advocated, we find meaning for our lives today, not just in a faraway future after death.

Jesus does not leave us alone with the vexing task of higher wakefulness, of knowing his love today in spite of the struggle to survive. He gave us stories and teachings to help us. To Jesus' words on wakefulness we turn next.

QUESTIONS FOR REFLECTION AND DISCUSSION

1. I defined faith as the knowledge that "a reliable Guide leads us on an adventurous journey toward a meaningful destination." What has been your greatest adventure? How was (or is) God a "reliable Guide" in that adventure?

2. While I accept Abraham Maslow's challenge to live beyond survival mode, I also accept Charles Darwin's warning that our animal nature limits us in doing so. Moreover, as Christians we believe that we cannot achieve higher wakefulness without God's help. What limitations of human nature suggest that we cannot achieve higher wakefulness on our own? When you consider your own times of higher wakefulness, how did God help you?

3. Death may be the most taboo topic in our culture. Yet, death figures prominently in the section "Three Levels of Wakefulness" in this chapter. Think of someone whose faith helped him or her

face death. That person may be someone you knew or a character in a story or drama. How did that person's life and way of facing death bear witness to God's power and love?

CHAPTER 2

keep Awake

THE DISTRACTION THAT FAILED

I can see them wide-eyed, a scruffy crew of country boys tentatively stepping down the streets of the big city, Jerusalem. Many of them grew up in open spaces where they could shout their names and hear the echo call back like a bantering angel. There they could see the sky and the whole rim of the horizon where morning sprouts up and returns to the earth at twilight. In the breeze by the Sea of Galilee, they could smell tomorrow's catch of fish.

Jesus and his disciples must have looked the part— a little too much hair, a little too plainly dressed, a little out of step, just enough off-center and just enough cautious bewilderment in their eyes to betray their origins in the hinterlands. The disciples never quite knew what to make of the crowds that followed Jesus in the country, but at least those crowds had one thing in mind—the power of Jesus, the authority of his teaching, and the wonder of his healing. But these people in Jerusalem had their own agendas, their own answers. They looked at the disciples in many ways, some with admiration, others with suspicion, still others with the condescending amusement of sophisticated urbanites sizing up a group of country bumpkins.

Jesus had already created a stir. He entered town on a donkey to an adoring crowd of fans who sang his praises and buzzed with hope for the kingdom he promised. Yet, rather than schmoozing with the high priests, he angrily overturned the vending booths in the temple's outer courts and drove out the merchants. He told off the scribes and Pharisees, calling them hypocrites, blind guides, and prophet-killers. The spotlight was getting hot, so the disciples tried to change the subject, do a little sight-seeing with Jesus.

"Look, Teacher, what large stones and what large buildings!" (Mark 13:1). Jesus used the spectacle of the skyline to issue a wake-up call. "Do you see these great buildings?" Jesus asked. "Not one stone will be left here upon another; all will be thrown down" (Mark 13:2). So much for the diversion.

With their anxiety now multiplied rather than divided, the disciples asked Jesus to tell them when the buildings will fall and how they can know when it is about to happen. At first, his response sounded like an answer: Many will claim to be saviors, offering quick fixes and sweet words. War will break out in many places, and worries of war will preoccupy people everywhere. Earthquakes will shatter cities, and famine will starve many.

The authorities will persecute Jesus' followers even as they spread the good news far and wide, good news in a world that seems to have no time for good news with all the bad news it produces. Jesus told them that they will find themselves in unspeakable situations, but the Holy Spirit will help them speak with the words they need. God's chosen ones will have to flee from home for safety. Everyone will work against them with lies. The creation itself will darken and threaten them. Then the Son of Man will come (Matthew 24:4-36; Mark 13:5-37; Luke 21:7-36).

Any time fits this description, from his own time to the destruction of the temple four decades later, from the dark ages to our own time of anxiety and threat. We see buildings fall, some in earthquakes in Kobe, Japan, or San Francisco, others in bomb blasts in Hiroshima or Oklahoma City. Many false saviors clamor for our attention, from corrupt televangelists to drug pushers, from political demagogues to peddlers of the latest get-rich-quick scheme. War rages without ceasing on the nightly news, in our streets, our homes, and our hearts. We have the resources to feed the world, but millions starve daily. The church suffers persecution where it is not tolerated, and it suffers trivialization where it is.

Some say Jesus pointed the disciples' gaze across two millennia to our age. Many see these passages along with other apocalyptic literature in the Bible as a code that, once cracked, reveals specific historical conditions forecasting the end of history. Such interpreters can claim a crucial piece of truth: Jesus indeed said that his return would follow all this chaos and horror.

However, they also deceive themselves and provide fodder for false prophets because Jesus himself concluded:

About that day or hour no one knows, neither the angels in heaven, nor the Son, but only the Father. Beware, keep alert; for you do not know when the time will come. It is like a man going on a journey, when he leaves home and puts his slaves in charge, each with his work, and commands the doorkeeper to be on the watch. Therefore, keep awake—for you do not know when the master of the house will come, in the evening, or at midnight, or at cockcrow, or at dawn, or else he may find you asleep when he comes suddenly. And what I say to you I say to all: Keep awake.

(Mark 13: 32-37)

Jesus meant his warning for all time, for his time and ours and the age to come. When the world seems to be going to hell in a hand basket, look. Keep awake. The kingdom of heaven is at hand.

Jesus did not answer the disciples when they asked, "Tell us, when will this be, and what will be the sign that all these things are about to be accomplished?" (Mark 13:4). He left them stewing in their angst, their feeling of dislocation, their self-conscious realization that they somehow did not belong there in Jerusalem with all the buildings and sophisticated people. He left them with the weight of their ignorance on their shoulders.

If they could not have a distraction, a meaningless discussion of the local architecture, Jesus could have at least given them the secret code to date the city's crumbling so they could have one up on the urban know-it-alls that made them feel so out of place. Jesus let them hang on to that sorry feeling because their sense of dislocation brought them closer to the truth than the feeling of being at home in Galilee fishing, making a home by the water.

Jesus knew that his disciples felt out of place in Jerusalem not because they were country hicks but because they were inevitably out of place wherever they went. They were citizens of a kingdom that was here but not yet here. They were pilgrims ever away from home, ever looking for a home, ever unsure what home looks like. They differed from the rest who made themselves feel at home in the shadow of the tall buildings and monolithic walls of the city. If they felt inferior, they need not have because the coming kingdom would stand sure and eternal, even more so than the hard stones at the corner of the temple.

So they must never resort to distractions. They must keep awake and watch.

What the Kingdom Looks Like

But watch for what? Watch where? Where does one look for another kingdom while the walls of Jerusalem still stand? Is it a kingdom without walls or tall buildings? A kingdom without streets?

The disciples did not get easy answers. Jesus did not lay out the street plan of the kingdom. He did not take them to the kingdom's capitol or visitor's center. He took them instead to the large upper room of an old house in the city to dine with them and to tell them good-bye.

In the upper room, Jesus took a few final cracks at answering the questions they pondered. He tried to show them what the kingdom looks like. For starters, he washed their feet. Stripped of his outer garment, he tied a towel around his waist, carried a bowl of water and a rag to every one of the twelve disciples, got down on his knees, scrubbed their calluses, wiped the dirt from between their toes, and gave them a quick foot massage for good measure (John 13:3-16).

In so doing he showed them that in God's kingdom, the king is servant of all. Only a short time before this day as they approached Jerusalem, he told them, "The greatest among you will be your servant. All who exalt themselves will be humbled, and all who humble themselves will be exalted" (Matthew 23:11-12). In the upper room, he repeated those words not by speaking, but by doing. Upon seeing humble, self-effacing service, watch closely. The kingdom is in sight.

He gathered them around the table for a meal. They had freshly baked bread, a gravy boat, and wine. John does not mention smoked trout or caviar or even homemade broccoli casserole. In the kingdom, it's not what one eats that counts. It's how one shares. It's how one keeps the company of others, passes the gravy, and waits for a friend to slowly chew and savor the bread between comments.

It's how one shares memories and makes memories in the common, creaturely act of eating. "Then he took a loaf of bread," Luke writes (22:19), "and when he had given thanks, he broke it and gave it to them, saying, 'This is my body, which is given for you. Do this in remembrance of me.'"

When people share time and food and memories, especially memories of Jesus sharing bread and wine, body and blood, look closely. The kingdom is as near as the salt shaker.

Jesus named his betrayer, Judas, and rather than rallying his friends to strangle the troublemaker, he picked out a choice piece of sweet, hot bread, dipped it in the gravy, and gave it to him. Then he sent him quietly on his way to do the dirty work while the rest chewed and chatted, scarcely realizing the difference. In the kingdom, nobody exercises power through force. They exercise it through love. They feed and protect their enemies (John 13:21-30).

Friends forgive each other in the kingdom. When Simon Peter declared his loyalty even unto death, Jesus responded, "Will you lay down your life for me? Very truly, I tell you, before the cock crows, you will have denied me three times" (John 13:38). Then he reached over and wiped some gravy from Peter's beard and continued speaking to Peter and the rest: "Do not let your hearts be troubled. Believe in God, believe also in me" (John 14:1). In the kingdom, we cannot disappoint each other enough to deplete the abundant forgiveness and hope the King provides.

Perplexed and worried by Jesus' allusions to his impending departure and his invitation to follow him to his Father's house, Thomas asked for a map to the place. Jesus said, "I am the way." Inspired by Thomas' bold query, Philip asked Jesus to show them the Father. Jesus said that since Philip had seen Jesus in action, he had seen more than he could comprehend of God in action. Furthermore, any time he sees himself or anyone else doing as Jesus does, he will see Jesus in action again (John 14:1-14). The kingdom comes whenever we get so caught up in Jesus' wondrous works that we begin to do them ourselves.

Yet, seeing Jesus is not as simple as it appears. People out there wanted to kill him. Even his own disciples would scatter when the going got tough. If anyone in that room or in Jerusalem or in Galilee really saw Jesus for who he was, he would not talk of going to another place to abide with the Father. The disciples would feel no peril, no angst, no feeling out of place in the city, no longing for a new home. One disciple asked, "Lord, how is it that you will reveal yourself to us, and not to the world?" (John 14:22). Seeing Jesus even as he stood there in the flesh, was no simple matter. So he took some time to teach them how to see him.

"Keep my commandments" (John 15:10), he taught them, and the commandments are this: "Love one another as I have loved you. No one has greater love than this, to lay down one's life for one's friends" (John 15:12). When they love others as he loved them, they will see him amid the beloved. When they love even unto death—which he will demonstrate personally in the horrible hours to come—they will see him in the suffering so clearly it will overcome their pain.

Jesus told them that the sense of displacement they felt on the street would get more pronounced, that they would see more clearly the distinction between the world and the kingdom. When the world spewed its wrath on him, they would see the distinction more clearly, and when the world attacked them, they would see it more clearly still. Often they would see him amid the suffering, but when they did not, they would not be alone. God would send a Helper, the Spirit of Truth, to get them through (John 15:18-16:15).

Strange as it seems, they would see the kingdom where they see suffering, his suffering, their friend's suffering, their own suffering. Suffering in this world opens a window to joy in the kingdom. "When a woman is in labor, she has pain, because her hour has come. But when her child is born, she no longer remembers the anguish because of the joy of having brought a human being into the world. So you have pain now; but I will see you again, and your hearts will rejoice, and no one will take your joy from you" (John 16:21-22).

JESUS' HIGH PRIESTLY PRAYER

The disciples looked puzzled and pained. All this teaching about his going away and being with them, this suffering to find joy, this hostile world through which the kingdom sprouts like flowers in the sidewalk made their eyes glaze over. He fared much better when he showed them pictures of the kingdom by washing their feet or giving them food. So he showed them one last thing, something they knew about and wondered about but seldom caught him in the act of doing out loud. He let them listen in on one of his personal prayers, one of his intimate talks with his Father.

"Father, the hour has come," he started. Every stomach knotted and every spine tingled in that place. His address to God held as many words of mystery as words of intimacy. He spoke of glory and eternity. He said that he lived with God in glory before the world itself existed, before the first morning or the first embrace or the first catch of fish (John 17:1-5).

In the kingdom, we pray intimately to a Father whose thoughts we cannot imagine, whose words we cannot speak.

He spoke of the disciples, and even more chilling, he made them sound like more than country bumpkins. Jesus said God gave them to him, as if God chose them from the fishing boats or the tax collection office or John the Baptist's remote place on the river Jordan. He said that they "kept [God's] word," that they knew Jesus and that he came from God. These words astonished them. With each passing moment, they seemed to know less of him, where he came from, and where he was going (John 17:6-10).

In the kingdom, we learn to our surprise that God chose us and that God long since planted the seeds of glory in us, however sinful or foolish we may be.

He spoke of returning to God and leaving them in the world, and he asked God to protect them. Jesus said, "They do not belong to the world" (John 17:16), but that seemed to mean something much different than the claim that they stood out like sharecroppers on Wall Street. He said that they possessed the truth, that they knew God's name, that they had God's word, and that the world would hate them for it. So he asked God to sanctify them even as they take the punishment the world will mete out.

In the kingdom, God builds us up even as the world tries to tear us down.

Then Jesus prayed for the world itself, the very world of which he spoke in such diabolical terms. Just as he saw through the disciples' sins and foibles to the glory planted in them, so he saw through the world's rebellion against God and to the fingerprint of God on every soul. Jesus asked the Father to open the world's eyes to the Son so that the world would share the glory, the word, the mystery, the calling. He asked God to do it through the disciples with the unkempt hair and wary expressions and unsophisticated manners, through the divine love that changed their lives and spills over to change the world (John 17:20-24).

Find the kingdom in the wide open spaces of the heart where there is room for everyone.

Jesus concluded his prayer, "Righteous Father, the world does not know you, but I know you; and these know that you have sent me. I made your name known to them, and I will make it known, so that the love with which you have loved me may be in them, and I in them" (John 17:25-26). In the kingdom, the love we share looks so much like God's love because it is God's love, filling us up, giving us a share in divine glory.

MUSTARD SEEDS

"Thy kingdom come," he taught them to pray one day on a hillside in the country. They prayed it daily ever since. Yet, not until that fateful day in the upper room, overhearing Jesus at prayer with his Father, did they realize that in all those daily prayers for a way to see the kingdom and live in it, they begged for a job to do. The world will see the kingdom through the way the disciples share the story and the truth of Jesus, through the way God makes them holy amid the suffering of this life, through their love for one another, and through the Christ in their eyes when they love the world.

So it is with all who pray, "Thy kingdom come," two millennia hence. In these interim centuries between Christ's ascension and his return to fully answer that prayer, those who most long for God to reveal the kingdom will themselves reveal it unawares. In this world's terms, they will usually appear small, insignificant. Yet, in God's kingdom, the fruit of their longing and watching and serving will yield countless blessings.

"The kingdom of heaven is like a mustard seed that someone took and sowed in his field; it is the smallest of all the seeds, but when it has grown it is the greatest of shrubs and becomes a tree, so that the birds of the air come and make nests in its branches" (Matthew 13:31), he told them one day as they walked the roads of Galilee. The kingdom seems small and insignificant, a seed buried underfoot in the sod by the roadside. Yet, those who watch and wait will live in its shade, taste its spice, and watch the birds thrive in it.

He used the metaphor again later, telling them that if they have faith the size of a mustard seed they can move mountains (Matthew 17:20) or transplant mulberry trees in the sea (Luke 17:6). The kingdom is like a mustard seed. Faith is like a mustard seed. Both seem small and insignificant, the kingdom buried in a world where the pursuit of power and pleasure and money seem to overwhelm self-giving love, faith buried in hearts filled with fear, lust, and envy. Yet where faith is, there is the kingdom, and where the kingdom is, there is faith.

The smallness and insignificance of a disciple does not mean we must disregard the disciple to see the kingdom. Our cue is to look to the disciple and other unlikely people and places for signs of the kingdom. Then we must look past the smallness and insignificance for the power of God at work. Even if we look in the mirror.

The kingdom takes root and grows here today, even if it is only the size of a mustard seed, no larger than the kernels of faith in our hearts. The kingdom has not yet blossomed to its full proportion and glory. Yet, Jesus likened finding it to finding a hidden treasure or pearl and joyfully giving up all one has to claim it (Matthew 13:44-46). It is that small, that wonderful, that compelling even now.

Nobody knows whether the disciples remembered those country teachings about the kingdom that day in the city. Perhaps it did not occur to them until their fateful visit to Jerusalem ended with all the horror of the crucifixion and all the wonder of the resurrection. On that day in the big city of Jerusalem, they did not know what mustard seeds lay scattered all about that they would later see sprouted to full glory. They did not know the treasures and pearls they had yet to find. They did not know what mustard seeds and treasures and pearls they were themselves in the sight of God. They knew they felt awkward, out of place, scared. And they knew to keep awake and watch.

Of course Jesus taught them much more about the kingdom in days gone by, and we know they eventually remembered those teachings because those displaced country boys kept talking about them until somebody wrote them down. They blossomed into a glorious memory that millions still share through scripture two thousand years later. We will share more of those memories in the pages to come. For now it is enough to remember how Jesus taught us to keep awake and watch for the kingdom, a kingdom that he taught us how to see with his words and deeds.

The glory of any kingdom is the king who abides in it and reigns over it. The wakeful and alert citizen keeps an eye out for the king's face. In times of celebration, they gather around that face, and in times of suffering, they hunger to see face to face with the king in anger or sorrow or hope. A surprise glimpse of that face in the coming and going of a day's routine makes the day suddenly memorable. In the next chapter, we will discuss our search for God's face.

QUESTIONS FOR REFLECTION AND DISCUSSION

1. Briefly review this chapter for the signs of the kingdom for which Jesus urged his disciples to keep awake and watch. List the signs of the kingdom that Jesus taught his disciples through word and deed. When and where did you observe any of these signs recently? Which of these signs did you observe during worship?

2. Jesus' words in Mark about the last days and in John's version of the Last Supper depict the world as an antagonistic place for those who follow him. How do you think the world differs from the kingdom of God? How do the life of discipleship and the objectives of the world come into conflict? What hope for the world does Jesus express in John 17:20-24?

3. Remember a time when you felt out of place as the disciples may have felt on the streets of Jerusalem. How did God seem absent? How did God intervene and open your eyes to the kingdom in your midst?

CHAPTER 3

Seeking God's Face

Paul traveled about the Gentile world trying to help people see God's face. He started churches because people tend to see God's face in the love they share in Jesus' name. Furthermore, Paul hoped that the churches would demonstrate that love for all their neighbors to see. Deep down everyone longs to see God's face, and glimpses of God's face amid a loving congregation will draw those with eyes to see in for a closer look. Paul told the story of Jesus everywhere he went to help people wake up and see what they always longed to see: the face of God.

Through most of Paul's ministry, he indirectly implied his purpose to help people see God's face. However, Paul made it explicit once during a layover in Athens while he waited for his next ride to Corinth. Athens, the great seat of Hellenistic culture, did not fit in Paul's strategic plan. Maybe Paul thought Athens with all its skeptics and self-appointed seers would take too much work.

A college sophomore reading about Paul's entry onto the stage in Athens might double check to make sure that she did not mistakenly take her Ancient

Philosophy notes in her New Testament notebook. Paul left behind the biblical story with its long roads and exiles and promised land, its still small voices and cries from the cross, its shadows, smoke, and shafts of blazing light. He found himself in the clear, breezy air of the civic center where the Stoics and Epicureans and every other philosopher matched wits. Luke tells us, "Now all the Athenians and the foreigners living there would spend their time in nothing but telling or hearing something new" (Acts 17:21). The Internet for ancients. The armchair philosopher's paradise.

Paul entered from a drama of flesh and blood into a marketplace of abstraction. There he stood waiting for his next ride to the coast. His mind buzzed with the good news of a carpenter whose debating skills rivaled the best in Athens, but who ultimately made his point by closing his mouth and letting our sins tell the ugly truth when we nailed him to a cross. There Paul stood in this grand leisurely square, ideas all about him, but flesh and blood on his mind.

His body still ached from his last beating. He traveled from place to place to spread the word that a crucified rural rabbi defied all logic and all known religion by rising from the grave, palpable, real, anything but abstract, anything but a clever idea. Paul replayed this drama everywhere he went, going straight to the synagogue and lovingly offending the most supremely religious citizens there, who then exacted a pound of flesh for his preposterous story. Yet, somehow, he left each place more alive than when he came, and he left more life there than he found when he first arrived.

So there he stood in Athens with its grand ideas but its religion so whimsical that he could scarcely offend anyone short of drawing grunts of disbelief from reclining, grape-sucking skeptics. They worshiped statues, toys made of wood or stone or sometimes gold or bronze. They worshiped manufactured likenesses of human or beast or both, and the Athenians built shrines to these idols as if their dumb mouths issued a great decree or as if their immobile limbs fought a great cosmic battle in forgotten ages past. These greatest minds of the western world practiced a primitive, contrived faith.

Yet, Paul saw a sparkle of life in it all. To Paul's mind, no descent into sin, survival mode, or silliness could separate them from the love of God in Christ their Lord, even if they did not have the foggiest idea that Christ Jesus was their Lord or even a real person. In the gentle murmur of tautologies and esoterica and riddles in that breezy square, Paul heard the whole creation groan in anticipation. He felt the wind of the Spirit.

So he opened his mouth and started to talk. The drama of the Bible intermingled with the abstractions of metaphysics. Plato and Moses met at last. And Plato was interested.

After all, Paul offered a new idea, at least to the ears of the philosophers. Some of them led him to the top of the hill and bade him speak loudly enough for all to hear. "Athenians, I see how extremely religious you are in every way. For as I went through the city and looked carefully at the objects of your worship, I found among them an altar with the inscription, 'To an unknown god.' What therefore you worship as unknown, this I proclaim to you" (Acts 17:22-23).

Of course they listened intently as any of us would to hear someone say they know our God, the one we cannot name, the one that all the preachers and teachers and writers of the world seem to talk around without getting to the point. We know that this God whom they do not name dwells with us because sometimes the four walls of home or office close in on us, and we search for something, someone. We get in the car and make a lame excuse to go somewhere. We walk the streets or the malls or the shore with a lonely ache. We say we're just hungry or tired or blue.

But we search for an unknown God. We leave monuments to this God where we wander. Maybe we buy something we do not need from a little shop to remind us of something special that did not happen there. We leave an extra large tip at the diner. We leave a tear soaking in the sidewalk.

So there on that hill stood Paul, a short man with bowed, muscular legs, his eyes lost beneath glistening baldness and behind a protruding, hooked nose. He declared in a strained, high-pitched voice[1] to those great truth seekers that this God has a name, a story. We cannot contain in our shrines or in our houses or in our philosophies this God who made heaven and earth. One can contain a god, but one cannot domesticate this unknown God. This God gave life and breath to all things, peopled the earth, set the boundaries of the nations. This God gave us this place and all the places and faces of our lives.

Why did this God create us mortals and set the whole cycle of life in motion? Why did God give mortals flesh and not just ideas? "So that they would search for God and perhaps grope for him and find him—though indeed he is not far from each one of us" (Acts 17:27).

We blush. This little man from the east knows our searches, our restlessness. He found our monuments. So he entices us with a truth too beautiful to face: Our restless search for this God is the reason we are here. We may not name this God of our own accord, but we find our name, our meaning in the search itself.

"'Come,' my heart says, 'seek his face!' Your face, LORD do I seek. Do not hide your face from me" (Psalm 27:8-9). That cry from Israel of ages past, Paul heard there in Athens That searching passion from the wilderness between Egypt and Jerusalem, Paul saw in the eyes of those masters of the intellectual search for truth. For that brief moment their lives revolved about the face of God and the kingdom.

They did not listen for long because soon enough they wrote off Paul's resurrection story. That story offended them not only because the notion of resurrection seems preposterous, but because Paul located God's face in a human being. Gods of stone and wood they could manage, and abstractions they could believe in, but an unmanageable man, a particular flesh and blood person did not match what they looked for with their pagan rituals and intricate, airy philosophies.

Moreover, Jesus Christ eludes us if we "spend [our] time in nothing but telling or hearing something new." We see God's human face most clearly when we roll up our sleeves and obey Jesus' commands to love our neighbor amid the sweat and tears of life together. One does not see God's face through a passive process like watching TV. Likewise abstract calculation does not open our eyes to the concrete presence of God in Christ. Obedient action conditions our vision to see God's face.

Doing and Seeing

To rise above survival mode, we must seek out God's kingdom in which God reigns and personal survival and security do not rule. This entails a higher way of seeing. In survival mode, we focus mainly on things that pertain to our comfort and security. In higher wakefulness, we focus on the reflection of God, the movement of Christ among things. We look for God's kingdom.

To see God's kingdom, we must live like we belong there. To live in God's kingdom, we must open our eyes to see it. Doing God's will helps us to see God's kingdom, and seeing God's kingdom helps us to do God's will. Doing helps us see, and seeing helps us do.

Who can doubt that seeing helps us do? If I see with my own two eyes a treasure in a field, I will spend all I have to buy that field and have the treasure. Seeing is believing, and believing is just one or two synapses from doing. That's common sense.

But the notion that doing helps us see does not fit our common sense notion of seeing. We think of seeing as a passive process. We simply open our eyes and let the interaction of light rays and our ocular equipment take over.

Yet, doing in order to see means that to see past the horizon, I must put one foot in front of the other. To see a baby smile, I must open my eyes and mouth wide and make goofy sounds. I can see beauty in my beloved well into old age as long as I do the hard work of loving her.

In order to see the kingdom of God, Jesus taught, humbly serve others. Enjoy the intimacy of eating together, of being human together. Share generously. Love your enemy. Forgive your friends when they disappoint you. Obey Jesus. Do not conform to this world, and remain hopeful even when it hurts. Pray intimately to God. Honor your calling. Then you will find God's kingdom in what otherwise seems like a godless world. In the center of God's kingdom, you will find God face-to-face, and your joy will be complete.

Paul's Lessons in Faith and Action

On a cold day in Jerusalem, young Saul stood clutching a mound of coats piled so high in his arms that he had to peek over the top to watch the action. He watched Stephen, a member of that renegade sect who claimed that their leader, Jesus, rose from the grave. Stephen crossed the line by thumbing his nose at the temple, the holiest shrine of the Jewish faith. So Saul, short and awkward with bad eyesight, held his fellow Pharisees' coats while they pummeled Stephen with stones.

It was a terrible sight. Stephen, a young man in his prime, crumpled under the rain of rocks and gazed skyward with a bizarre joy in his dimming eyes as if looking into the eyes of his beloved. But this did not faze Saul. When called to protect and defend the law and traditions of God's very own chosen people, no ugliness or cruelty outweighed the virtue of keeping out the riffraff.

Besides, Saul cared little about seeing. He only wanted to stand in the right company when God sets the record straight once and for all, exalting Jerusalem and putting Rome in its place. Not that Saul had that much against Rome: He reaped the benefits of his Roman citizenship whenever prudent. But he knew Caesar's benefits ended with death, while God promised a kingdom of power beyond imagining and survival beyond the grave.

So he did all the right things. He obeyed the laws of ritual and moral purity to the letter. He did it not to see the kingdom but to earn the kingdom, to make a rightful claim to his place at God's table. He stored up brownie points for the day of reckoning like a squirrel gathering acorns amid the falling leaves of autumn.

Saul did not pursue this religious survival mission selfishly. If anyone like the Christians spread a false teaching to lead the common folk astray, he helped out by arranging more stonings. He offered to hold the coats. He found his calling that day in Jerusalem as bloody and broken Stephen gave up the ghost.

At least, that's what he thought until something happened on the road to Damascus, where he intended to cleanse the Jews of some Christian sludge in their midst. The risen Christ visited him in person, bowling him over in a dazzling sheet of light. "Why do you persecute me?" Jesus asked (Acts 9:4). At once Saul knew that the risen Christ appeared countless times before in the blood and bone and open eyes of Stephen and all the rest he watched suffer unto death. All along as he held the coats and heard the cries of the dying, he saw and heard the very Jesus whose living presence he denied and fought with all the violence his soul could muster.

Christ renamed him Paul and then ordered him to go to Damascus and get his new orders. In his new mission, Paul would serve Christ, the Christ he would see on the highways and byways, in the hulls of storm-tossed ships, in the musty darkness of prisons, and in the angry and weeping throngs of city streets. This Christ whom he crucified in those very same places now promised to pursue him, always before him, never letting him turn his head.

There by the road to Damascus, the light dimmed, leaving a thin cloud of dust as Paul's companions stood by blanched and wide-eyed. Paul stumbled to his feet, blind as a bat, the afterimage of that light and that face emblazoned permanently in his memory. He could not shake it. Seeing takes on a whole new significance for the blind, and Christ did not restore his sight until Paul was ready to see— really see—for the first time.

Doing also took on a whole new meaning for Paul. He retained his hope for God's coming in glory, but now he knew that the drama to fulfill that hope had already started and nobody had consulted him. His drive to do the right thing by the book amounted to nothing more than a religious survival scheme while the promised Messiah awakened his humble followers to life in the kingdom today.

They did not deserve it. They did not know the law like Paul did, nor did they do it as compulsively and meticulously as he. Nevertheless, they seemed as concerned as Paul to do the right thing, to obey God. Jesus, Paul learned, constantly called for obedience. But doing was not a matter of piling up brownie points for them. Rather, it was a matter of opening their eyes to see. If they loved their neighbor, they would see Christ in their neighbor. If they loved their enemy, they would see Christ there too, not to mention the outside chance that their enemy would see Christ in them. Doing helped them see the face of God, and seeing the face of God rewarded them sufficiently, the kingdom already come in their midst, the answer to their Lord's prayer.

Before his conversion, Paul joined his fellow Pharisees in doing righteous things for wrong-headed reasons—to maximize their security and survive when God takes over in the end. Their religious understanding, however sublime and storied, took them no further than the squirrel gathering food and watching vigilantly for threats. Fear motivated them more than faith.

After his conversion, Paul and his fellow Christians did righteous things in order to see God's face, to keep one another awake to God's face, and to open the world's eyes to God's face. They approached everything they did with the faith that Christ walked with them, suffered with them, and rejoiced with them, that every act of obedience revealed God already reigning in their midst. Faith amounts to more than believing without proof. It requires putting oneself on the line, casting aside all former sources of security to plunge ever deeper into a loving relationship with God. It means performing each act with the trust that God's hand is at work in the action and that obedience conditions us to see God more clearly.

From that day on the Damascus road until Nero killed him in Rome, Paul devoted himself to making sure the church never forgot these wonders of faith and action. God justifies us by grace through faith, he repeated like a broken record whenever someone tried to sell the churches a new scheme to earn God's rewards. He refused to let anyone drag them back down to the squirrel level of foraging and scheming for their ultimate survival. Jesus Christ took care of their survival and so much more when he died on the cross. Obey him and see his face.

LOVING AND KNOWING

Atop Mount Sinai, Moses popped the question to God, the question the Athenians wanted to ask, the question all of us want to ask in our searching: Will you show me your face? "You cannot see my face; for no one shall see me and live," God answered (Exodus 33:20). Then God passed in front of Moses to depart from the mountain, shielded Moses' view, but let Moses see the back that carries us all.

So what shall we make of all this talk about seeing God's face? I can see the print on this page, the light switch on the wall, the watch on my wrist, the blue sky out the window. But I certainly cannot see God in the same way. Skeptics say I cannot see God plainly because God does not exist and nothing else that escapes my five senses exists. Believers say I cannot see God plainly because God in infinite mercy does not annihilate us with more glory than we can bear. Either way, this talk of seeing God's face seems suspect to common sense. What does it mean?

Several millennia after Moses, Philip popped the question again during Jesus' farewell chat with his disciples. "'Lord, show us the Father, and we will be satisfied.' Jesus said to him, 'Have I been with you all this time, Philip, and you still do not know me? Whoever has seen me has seen the Father'" (John 14:8-9). We see God's face in the face of Christ.

And we do not survive the seeing, by the way. It kills us. Our old self dies, and a new self lives. Hence, Paul's peculiar words to the Colossians on higher wakefulness: "Set your minds on things above, not on earthly things. For you died, and your life is now hidden with Christ in God" (Colossians 3:2-3, NIV). For some the dying of the old self and the generation of the new happen in a dramatic flash like bitter, miserly Scrooge awakening with the Christmas spirit after a night of shattering dreams. For most of us it takes time and lots of doing, the kind of doing that helps us to see.

This doing that helps us to see is love. The Hebrews used the same term for the intimacy of husband and wife that they used for knowledge. Loving and knowing are inseparable.

The reward for acts of obedience to Christ's commands brings us the reward of seeing Christ, God's human face. What do Christ's commands boil down to? "You shall love the Lord your God with all your heart, and with all your soul, and with all your mind, and with all your strength. . . . [and] You shall love your neighbor as yourself" (Mark 12:30-31). Love for God and love for neighbor opens our eyes to see

God's face in our neighbor and beyond. There the resurrected Christ lives for us to love, to know, to see.

Of the final day of blessing and judgment, Jesus taught:

> Then the king will say to those at his right hand, "Come, you that are blessed by my Father, inherit the kingdom prepared for you from the foundation of the world; for I was hungry and you gave me food, I was thirsty and you gave me something to drink, I was a stranger and you welcomed me, I was naked and you gave me clothing, I was sick and you took care of me, I was in prison and you visited me." Then the righteous will answer him, "Lord, when was it that we saw you hungry and gave you food, or thirsty and gave you something to drink? And when was it that we saw you a stranger and welcomed you, or naked and gave you clothing? And when was it that we saw you sick or in prison and visited you?" And the king will answer them, "Truly I tell you, just as you did it to one of the least of these who are members of my family, you did it to me."
>
> (Matthew 25:34-40)

To the humble, common sense question, "When did we see you," Jesus answered in so many words, "You saw me when you loved."

I can go no further than this toward making common sense of the notion of seeing God's face.

Ultimately, how God's face appears amid the suffering and the beloved mystifies me. Why God chooses to appear to us in this context baffles even the most learned or religious. Only loving acts performed with faith in God's presence will prepare us to see the mysterious face.

Paul eventually made it from Athens to Corinth, and there in Corinth, he taught them how to see the face of God. He did so by teaching them about Jesus Christ and Christ's love. He did so by loving the Corinthian church—a church that was hard to love. They distorted the gospel in every way they could and seemed headstrong on religions of security and survival rather than Jesus' religion of life in the kingdom now. Moreover, they questioned Paul's authority and constantly challenged his credibility in spite of his self-giving love for them.

To this church Paul wrote perhaps the greatest hymn on love ever written, 1 Corinthians 13. Pick up your Bible and read it. No paraphrase will do. As you see, he tells them that their good actions, no matter how spectacular, will leave them empty without love. He characterizes love as patient, kind, humble, calm, forgiving. It "rejoices in the truth" (v. 6).

All other ways to truth will pass away, but not love. All of our current knowledge is incomplete: "For we know only in part, and we prophesy only in part; but when the complete comes, the partial will come to an end" (vv. 9-10). Even our knowledge through love is incomplete, unfinished, but love will carry us to the ultimate knowledge in the end: "Now we see in a mirror, dimly, but then we will see face to face. Now I know only in part; then I will know fully, even as I have been fully known" (v. 12).

Then we will see face to face with God. We will know God intimately as God has known us all along. God's face is here, now. God's kingdom thrives all about us. But we see only in glimpses. The limits to our vision are the limits to our love. To those limits we turn in the next chapter.

QUESTIONS FOR REFLECTION AND DISCUSSION

1. Read 1 Corinthians 13. Think of someone you know who embodies well the characteristics of love in verses 4-7. How might that person describe his or her knowledge of God? How might that person deal with the fact that he or she knows God "only in part?"

2. Read Matthew 25:31-40. Remember a time when you helped someone in need. Describe that person's face as you helped him or her. What does that face tell you about the face of Christ?

3. Before his conversion, Paul persecuted the church. During Paul's conversion, Jesus identified with the persecuted ones by asking Paul, "Why do you persecute me?" (Acts 9:4). Recall a time when you persecuted Christ. How did Jesus move you from that event or condition to one of greater love and greater closeness to God?

CHAPTER 4

Turning Around

ANXIOUS DREAMS

My dog has a rich dream life. A yellow Labrador retriever, she lives for the chase, and many nights after the lights go out, my wife and I hear her issue muffled yips and barks on the floor beside the bed. Her legs twitch, her eyes dance, and her body tightens. In her dreams, I suspect she chases a deer she saw earlier in the day, or she wards off a trespasser. She probably gets food in the process.

I can only imagine what she dreams or whether she dreams at all. For all I know, her slumbering barks and twitches amount to nothing more than the physiological responses I observe. I know even less about the sleep of squirrels, whether they dream, and what they dream about. Taking my cue from Darwin, I suspect that it does not totally differ from what happens when I sleep.

I dream of taking flight from diabolical predators, as I suspect the squirrel does. However, I also dream that I am back in school and that I forgot about an exam. Occasionally, I dream about a day at work in which everything seems fine except that I forgot my pants. Those anxious dreams seem roughly akin to the squirrel's flight dreams. Most of my dreams, however, make no immediate sense as I drift from one unrelated setting to another, encountering characters from my distant past along with my daily acquaintances, and we exchange idiosyncratic words and emotions. I envy people whose dreams have clear plots.

A psychoanalyst might enjoy helping me with my problem, showing me the symbolic relations between the absurd mix of elements in my dreams. But I find waking dreams more interesting. They tell me more about how I rise above the squirrel's level of existence and how I fall back into it.

Waking dreams include all my imaginings from fantasies to aspirations. As I sort through them, I struggle to give a focus to my life. This process often seems as plotless as my night dreams. I hold tenaciously to silly lusts along with visions of ambitious adventure, or I dismiss noble projects with the same casual sweep of the hand with which I discard junk mail.

We cannot live all the lives we imagine before death claims us. We must make choices. With each choice we move ahead, becoming someone new in our successes and failures, seeing things we never before saw, waking up. We also leave behind a dream with each choice, and we grieve the loss.

In the preceding chapters, we allowed Jesus and his servant Paul to lead us in the construction of dreams that correspond to the reality of God's kingdom and the presence of God's face. In the upper room, Jesus gently and imaginatively equipped his disciples to set aside their old dreams of who he was and what kind of world to hope for. He gave them new images of himself and his kingdom: the washing of feet, the sharing of bread, praying, dying, rejoicing amid suffering. He gave them a new image of God's face just by calling them by name and getting them to look him in the eye.

By faith we believe that God's reign is more than just a dream. It is reality. Yet, we only seem to catch it in glimpses. Most of our lives we live in between visits to the kingdom. If we practice spiritual discipline, our prayers and Bible readings and songs and silences keep us watchful for the kingdom, but we do not hear its music just yet. We hear all of creation groaning in anticipation of it, and our prayers only seem to blend in with the collective groan that rises into the cold darkness of outer space. If we do not practice a regular life of prayer or meditation, God's face occasionally arrests us, but in between those epiphanies we live in the desert of our routines. Our restlessness is our prayer.

Doing helps us see, we learned in chapter 3, but the more diligently we seek the kingdom, the more painfully aware we become of our moral inertia. Paul's exasperated statement speaks for us all: "I do not understand my own actions. For I do not do what I want, but I do the very thing I hate" (Romans 7:15). Paul felt the frustration. In spite of his travels and sermons and healings and whippings and imprisonments, Paul too hit the wall of his own sin and could not see past it without help. He did more than most of us in obedience to Christ, so he saw more of

Christ than most of us will ever see. But in the end, he too saw in a glass darkly.

One wonders whether we can attain our ideal dream of the kingdom. Earlier we read Jesus' dream of the kingdom: He sets apart the sheep and blesses them for having served him as they served the suffering people in their midst. In their service, they stood face-to-face with him, unawares. Yet, Jesus couples this good dream of his sheep's fate with a nightmare about those goats who do nothing:

> Then he will say to those at his left hand, "You that are accursed, depart from me into the eternal fire prepared for the devil and his angels; for I was hungry and you gave me no food, I was thirsty and you gave me nothing to drink, I was a stranger and you did not welcome me, naked and you did not give me clothing, sick and in prison and you did not visit me." Then they also will answer, "Lord, when was it that we saw you hungry or thirsty or a stranger or naked or sick or in prison, and did not take care of you?" Then he will answer them, "Truly I tell you, just as you did not do it to one of the least of these, you did not do it to me." And these will go away into eternal punishment, but the righteous into eternal life.
>
> (Matthew 25:41-46)

That makes me feel like a goat every time I read it. For each time I see Christ in the suffering of my brothers and sisters and respond with compassionate action, I can count ten times that I screen out the sight of a hungry face or the sound of a lonely cry. I could write a nice little term paper on my good deeds which Christ answered with the sight of his loving face. Yet, the Library of Congress could not hold the list of my sins of omission and the many times Christ stood before me with open arms as I walked on by. Too spiritually drowsy to listen, I scarcely hear him behind me asking the question that he first asked in the hour of his betrayal: "Could you not keep awake one hour? Keep awake and pray that you may not come into the time of trial; the spirit indeed is willing, but the flesh is weak" (Mark 14:37-38).

Paul wrote, "Now if I do what I do not want, it is no longer I that do it, but sin that dwells within me. . . . For I delight in the law of God in my inmost self, but I see in my members another law at war with the law of my mind, making me captive to the law of sin that dwells in my members" (Romans 7:20, 22-23). If Paul's talk of the resurrection of the body made the ancient Athenians walk away shaking their heads and scoffing, this talk of sin makes modern Americans do the same. It violates our most cherished dreams about ourselves. The notion of our captivity to sin that dwells in our members violates our dreams of ourselves as the free and the brave. Moreover, it sounds downright judgmental, and it does not do much for our self-esteem.

Nevertheless, just as the resurrected Christ came back to haunt the Athenian world and replaced its dreams, so the Christ who conquers sin must come back and haunt us, overthrowing our dreams and replacing them with the reality of the kingdom. Otherwise, we slumber. We miss the face we long to see.

RECOGNIZING SIN

Many people view sin as any action from a list of bad behaviors written by God or tradition or a mysterious, wise ancestor. Cheating on one's spouse. Drinking too much. Stealing from the cookie jar. Sin, by this definition, is anything one might reasonably expect a ten-year-old boy to do if left unattended for too long.

It's the breaking of rules and conventions of decent conduct. We can confess this kind of sin because we also believe there would be something wrong with us if we did not commit such indiscretions occasionally. We come before God like a kid facing Dad when he comes home from work and hears Mom's stern report. Dad lectures us and perhaps metes out punishment, but we know that Dad is glad we're normal.

When we view sin this way, we can also distinguish between the sins normal kids like us commit and the sins that truly bad people commit. The evening news flashes images of the mail bomber, the wife slasher, the tyrannical dictator, the terrorist, the woman who drowned her children. We shake our heads in disbelief and moralize. These ugly images offer perverse comfort because our own childish sins seem so insignificant when compared to these horrors.

How do we perceive sin? When viewed from the perspective above, we see sin the way an IRS agent sees a tax return. Scrutinize the details. Listen cynically. Don't let down your guard; don't get soft. If they don't have written proof, don't believe it. Penalize in proportion to the error, and add interest.

Obviously, we recognize such sin much more easily in others than in ourselves. Few practice the self-denial necessary to size up one's own moral tax return rigorously and honestly. One can do it, and when done effectively, it can help. The Twelve Steps of Alcoholics Anonymous include such a moral inventory of oneself, and the successful inventory usually results in a more sober, loving, and spiritually awake self. Yet, it often takes a revoked driver's license, a failed marriage, or a lost job to motivate such a walk through the fire.

In fact, successful recovering alcoholics generally see sin in a more profound sense than the sum total of their behavioral boo-boos. Because so many people view sin in such a simplistic and judgmental fashion, most recovering alcoholics do not use the term sin, not because it disturbs them too much but because it does not disturb them enough. Recovering alcoholics first and most starkly recognize sin when they see their broken self looking back at them in the mirror. They see a stranger in that reflection. They see someone with whom they would not spend fifteen minutes and realize that they have to spend the rest of their lives with that person.

They see someone cut off from family and friends and God for the sake of a drink. They see unmanageable chaos of their lives and their inability to take control. They see the mail bomber, the abuser, the tyrant, the murderous mother, and they see someone who could be themselves, so horrified are they with what they have done with their lives.

They know sin for what it really is. But it takes some time before they are ready to do the inventory. They need to learn another lesson in how to see sin.

A rich young man ran up to Jesus, clutching his moral inventory in one hand and holding his hat with the other. Almost out of breath, he asked, "What must I do to inherit eternal life?" Jesus ran through the rules with him: Don't murder, don't commit adultery, don't steal, don't lie, don't cheat, and treat your parents right. Waving his moral inventory under Jesus' nose, he said, "Teacher, I have kept all these since my youth"(Mark 10:17-20).

Jesus did not bring out the moral tax code at that point. He did not need an inventory to see the young man's sin. Mark tells us, "Jesus, looking at him, *loved him* and said, 'You lack one thing; go, sell what you own, and give the money to the poor, and you will have treasure in heaven; then come, follow me'" (Mark 10:21, emphasis mine). Jesus undeniably saw the depth of the young man's sin—his addictive dependence on possessions—and it took looking at him and loving him to see it. We cannot see sin clearly until we see it through the eyes of love.

The recovering alcoholic cannot do the moral inventory without first becoming immersed in the caring fellowship of fellow alcoholics who want not to drink. Moreover, the recovering alcoholic must accept God's offer to restore sanity in the alcoholic's life, to take charge with divine, healing love. Only engulfed in such love can the recovering alcoholic look in the mirror and see straight.

So it is with all of us. The alcoholic's hard lessons in sin apply to everyone. Some affirm this because all of us have an addiction of some sort, an addiction to work or golf or television or gossip or money or anything else we allow to dominate our time and attention. The language of addiction is modern America's secular language for idolatry, that most basic of all sins. The first commandment reads, "I am the LORD your God, who brought you out of the land of Egypt, out of the house of slavery; you shall have no other gods before me" (Exodus 20:2). The one God who sets us free will not tolerate our self-enslavement to some substitute.

So our Lord calls all of us, like the alcoholic, to name our idols and walk away from them into the arms of the only God who desires for us to be free. All are akin to the recovering alcoholic not only because we have our idols, but because we have a loving God ever at our heels to whom we can always turn to get our freedom back. Until then we live in survival mode because our idols seduce us with shallow promises to protect us from the inevitable pain of living. They keep us scurrying for security, scrambling for a fix, hoarding for the winter, no time to love.

Knowing our dreams helps us to name our idols. Can I dream of the kingdom without imagining myself having a place of high standing there? If not, I worship status. Does the kingdom include a new Mercedes every year? If so, I worship wealth. In the kingdom, do I win God's accolades through high achievement in the angel corps? If I imagine as much, I worship work. We find the kingdom hard to imagine because we have such difficulty leaving our gods behind. Wakeful awareness of the kingdom requires God's help in leaving the idolatrous baggage of our dreams behind.

REPENTANCE

> Therefore say to the house of Israel, Thus says the Lord GOD: Repent and turn away from your idols; and turn away your faces from all your abominations. For any . . . who separate themselves from me, taking their idols into their hearts and placing their iniquity as a stumbling block before them . . . I the LORD will answer them myself. I will set my face against them; I will make them a sign and a byword and cut them off from the midst of my people; and you shall know that I am the LORD.
>
> (Ezekiel 14:6-8)

Hear the growl in these words, a growl from a mother bear injured by her beloved cub. The prophet reveals how sin stirs up divine pain and anger: It separates us from God. As long as we give ourselves to lesser gods, we have no time for the one true God, and we certainly have no time to open ourselves to other creatures made in God's image.

The Hebrew term for "repent," *shub*, literally translates, "to turn around."[1] Go back to the one you abandoned. Pour out your heart. Admit your sin. Make peace.

Someone had to awaken ancient Israel so it could see the Messiah when he came. God chose a wild man. John the Baptist stood in the River Jordan far out in the hinterlands, out there among the gnats and the heat and the dust. He wore camel skin. He ate locusts and wild honey. He did not cry, "Boy, have I got a deal for you!" or "Try Dr. John's sassafras serum for a newer, younger you!" He cried, "Repent, for the kingdom of heaven has come near" (Matthew 3:2), and the people came from far and wide as if he were giving away money.

They came, rich and poor, male and female, wading out to John. Scripture only tells us of John's baptizing and preaching to them, but I imagine him also listening. I can see the people spilling their hearts, telling their tales of one sin leading to ten more, of lives so immersed in sin that they could scarcely breathe without digging themselves deeper in it. They told of their gods—sex, status, money, ego, fine things, sleazy things, work, leisure, and many more—and John could see the weight of these gods on their shoulders. He listened until they named every god and spilled every remorseful emotion.

Then he took their heads in his big, callused hands and looked them in the eyes long and hard. I suspect he spoke tenderly to some, prayed fervently with others. Some he chided, I suspect, drawing from them a fuller confession, struggling with them until they held nothing back. With others still, perhaps, he said nothing at all, only looked long into their eyes and listened with them to the terrible silence of God.

He guided their heads under water and held them for a moment. With that motion a miracle occurred. The gods washed away. The whole inventory of sins dissipated in the air about John like the mist over the water when the morning sun hovers over the hill. It was a kind of death, this person who had no identity apart from those gods, now crouched under water, practically weightless, cleansed of the terrible burden of that old identity.

Finally, John lifted their faces into the air above the Jordan. Although they looked the same, they surfaced as new people, free and light as air. Gasping for breath, feeling the cool breeze against their wet skin, they were awake. For the first time ever, awake.

It was repentance from start to finish. Hearing the news about the wild man at the Jordan and making the decision to go. Taking the long walk, sizing up one's life with each plodding step. Hearing his cries from a distance, and fearfully walking to the river bank. Waiting one's turn. Then stepping in, confessing all the way until eye to eye with the confessor, looking for God's face in his, seeing only John but knowing that God's power seethes there in the water, in the air, in the eyes. Dying and awakening again, a new person, finally awake.

Two thousand years later, some catch planes and go to the Jordan where a kind and bold pastor baptizes pilgrims. Some go to a church that baptizes by immersion. But most of us, if we ever awaken at all, hear of this distant wildness, and one morning we make a decision, a quiet, seemingly small one. We walk for days or years, all of our coming and going and searching amounting to that journey to the River Jordan. We taste the loneliness from years of living with gods who offer everything but true intimacy with the one God, our families, our neighbors, our selves. Leaving our dreams behind, we find the right place or time, the right face, the right voice, the wildness, and we confess. We let the gods wash away. At last we wake up.

Some remember this as one discreet event that happened in Cleveland one hot August night or on the road to El Paso on Christmas Eve. Many others remember it as a whole life's story, a process from birth to death, a lifetime of searches and confessions and baptisms, a lifelong repentance. However it happens, we live our lives amid promises and spiritual teachings that sound inspiring, ethereal, serene, but which ultimately amount to fairy tales until we face the reality of our sin, take up our crosses, and let our old selves die.

THE MORNING AFTER

After repentance, we are new, and we may revel in the flush of new life for a while. Yet, the gods do not give up on us that easily. They work their way back into our dreams.

Many scholars contend that Paul's confession quoted earlier—"I do not do what I want, but I do the very thing I hate" (Romans 7:15)—is a depiction of life before wakefulness, before repentance and cleansing and new life. Indeed it is. Yet, I must side with those who contend that it applies also to life after awakening and becoming new. "So then with my mind I am a slave to the law of God, but with my flesh I am a slave to the law of sin" (Romans 7:25), he concludes, confessing the ambiguity of all of our lives.

The Holy Spirit changes us; yet, we remain the same. We worship the one true God; yet, other gods pull us in every direction. We dream a new dream, but the old ones seep into our fantasies. We awaken, but only in fits and starts, like someone coming out of a coma.

God seems to live in paradox. God is present, yet sometimes painfully absent. We see God's face; yet, God is hidden. We hear God's word; yet, God is silent.

We live in the kingdom, but the kingdom remains yet to come. When we repent and open our eyes to the kingdom, we see wonderful new things, but only in precious glimpses. Christ conquered sin, leaving it like a smashed hornet's nest. Sin lacks the home base to sustain itself over the long haul, but it stings us and harasses us all the more in the meantime.

Our own initiative will not fulfill our fondest dreams of the kingdom regardless of how fiercely we attack the idols in our dreams. Wakefulness offers no psychological technique whereby we enter sinless bliss. We must wait for God and learn how to wait well. Wakefulness requires skillful waiting, and such waiting with constant attention to small intimations of the kingdom brings a joy all its own. That joy makes the Christian life worth pursuing even as the inertia and confusion and darkness of life continue to dog us. To the meaning of the waiting and the promise of the joy we turn in the next chapter.

QUESTIONS FOR REFLECTION AND DISCUSSION
1. Equipped with a pad and pen, watch your least favorite television show. List every image or theme

expressed on the show (including commercials) that people may worship as idols. Now watch your favorite television show and make the same kind of list. How do the lists differ? How are they the same? Which list was more difficult to make and why?

2. Many people identify with Paul's confession, "I do not understand my own actions. For I do not do what I want, but I do the very thing I hate" (Romans 7:15). Remember a time when you felt that frustration. How did God help you to cope with it? If you resisted God's help (as we all do at times), how did you resist?

3. In *Addiction and Grace*, Dr. Gerald May reflects on his many years of treating addictions and writes: "I . . . learned that all people are addicts, and that addictions to alcohol and other drugs are simply more obvious and tragic addictions than others have. To be alive is to be addicted, and to be alive and addicted is to stand in need of grace."[2] Most of us know a story of someone who recovered from an addiction. How do you identify with that person's struggle? How did that person's experience of God's grace resemble your own? If you are studying this book in a group, share the story with the others (disguising the identity of the person if appropriate) and allow them to address those questions.

CHAPTER 5

waiting for God

RADICAL WAITING

From the River Jordan, from the city streets, from the awakening heart, a cry rings out:

> Out of the depths I cry to you, O LORD;
> > O LORD, hear my voice.
> Let your ears be attentive
> > to my cry for mercy.
>
> If you, O LORD, kept a record of sins,
> > O LORD, who could stand?
> But with you there is forgiveness;
> > therefore you are feared.
> > > (Psalm 130:1-4, NIV)

One may repent however one wishes, with a stammer, an apology, an inventory of sins. The psalmist here shows us that we may also repent with joy, with adoration, with song. In the same melody and mood, the psalmist moves us beyond repentance to waiting:

I wait for the LORD, my soul waits,
  and in his word I put my hope.
My soul waits for the LORD
  more than watchmen wait for
  the morning,
  more than watchmen wait for
  the morning.

         (vv. 5-6, NIV)

This song sounds strangely sweet to modern ears. Joy colors this pining. Beauty adorns this incompleteness. Waiting, of all things, fills the heart and stirs the singer to visions of a new tomorrow:

O Israel, put your hope in the LORD,
  for with the LORD is unfailing love,
  and with him is full redemption.
He himself will redeem Israel
  from all their sins.

         (vv. 7-8, NIV)

How can anyone speak of waiting in such hopeful and happy tones? We do not tolerate a five-minute wait for a burger and fries. We cannot bear the loss of precious minutes as we wait for the check-out clerk to change the roll of receipt paper. Heaven is a personal computer that calls up files in fewer milliseconds than last year's model. Hell is creeping rush-hour traffic.

Having walked on the moon and split the atom, we begrudge death's stubborn persistence, so we race against the final deadline it imposes, leaning on our car horns and stuffing our fax machines so we can have more time to do as we please. Few remember a world in which everything depended on rains that fall when they fall, on letting the watermelon take its sweet time to ripen, on the wisdom of old age.

If waiting for the light to turn green makes us crazy, how can waiting for God make us serene? Yet, it must. Technology will never touch the necessity of training our souls to wait.

"My soul waits for the LORD more than watchmen wait for the morning, more than watchmen wait for the morning," the psalmist sings above the din of the streets and phones and printers. These words ebb and flow with the graceful necessity of the tide. This song is background noise to lower wakefulness. Higher wakefulness dances to its tune.

"Consider the ravens: they neither sow nor reap, they have neither storehouse nor barn, and yet God feeds them. Of how much more value are you than the birds! And can any of you by worrying add a single hour to your span of life? If then you are not able to do so small a thing as that, why do you worry about the rest?" (Luke 12:24-26). The music continues, just as melodious and serene. Yet, the words sting the modern mind. They totally contradict the way we live. Why must this song issue from Jesus Christ? Why not from some radio talk show host so we can write it off as clever propaganda?

"Consider the lilies, how they grow:" his song continues, "they neither toil nor spin; yet I tell you, even Solomon in all his glory was not clothed like one of these. But if God so clothes the grass of the field, . . . how much more will he clothe you—you of little faith!" (Luke 12:27-28). Even "you of little faith" sounds like music. Must Jesus torture us with a beauty we cannot attain?

What would we do with ourselves without anxiety over what we will eat or what we will wear? How would we fill the void left if we relinquished our anxious striving?

Jesus sings on as if he does not hear the question, but he answers it in the final lines: "And do not keep striving for what you are to eat and what you are to drink, and do not keep worrying. For it is the nations of the world that strive after all these things, and your Father knows that you need them. Instead, strive for his kingdom, and these things will be given to you as well" (Luke 12:29-31).

Strive first for the kingdom of God. Wake up. Open your eyes. It is right before you, he seems to say. You miss it in your hurry. The kingdom will fill with treasures the void that you otherwise fill with futility: "Do not be afraid, little flock, for it is your Father's good pleasure to give you the kingdom. Sell your possessions, and give alms. Make purses for yourselves that do not wear out, an unfailing treasure in heaven, where no thief comes near and no moth destroys. For where your treasure is, there your heart will be also" (Luke 12:32-34).

God gives the treasure from above, but a task lies before us: giving up our attachments, sharing what we have, making space in our hearts for gifts that last. Learning the discipline of waiting without worry. Everywhere we turn, the commercial world lures us to new attachments, seducing us to believe that we need what we did not need before. Look out for number one, conventional wisdom teaches.

Waiting without worry seems impossible in such a competitive world.

So waiting for God is no sentimental notion that we can cross-stitch in mauve lettering, frame, and hang on the bedroom wall. It is a radical, counter-cultural teaching. It takes grit. Jesus continues in Luke 12:35-48 with an analogy between those who wait and slaves who keep a master's house in his absence. Those who wait well do their tasks diligently and remain ever ready to greet the master. "You too must stand ready because the Son of man is coming at an hour you do not expect" (v. 40, NJB).

But those who lose discipline in the absence of the master, who abuse the other slaves and drink up half the wine cellar will get caught in the act when the master returns. "His master will come on a day he does not expect and at an hour he does not know. The master will cut him off and send him to the same fate as the unfaithful" (v. 46, NJB). Watchful waiting for God demands all of our attention, all of our heart, all of our nerve, all of our time. We cannot save it for bedtime or quiet time. In everything we do at home, at work, on the highway, in the polling booth, at the mall, and in the church, we must watchfully wait for God.

MYTHS ABOUT WAITING FOR GOD

No football coach ever wrote, "Wait for God," in the playbook. No scientist ever wrote, "Wait for God," in the lab manual. No general ever wrote, "Wait for God," in the battle plans. No salesman ever wrote, "Wait for God," in the list of sure sales tactics. No corporate executive ever wrote, "Wait for

God," in employees' job descriptions or on the stockholders' prospectus.

The coach, scientist, general, salesman, and CEO seek a competitive edge in order to achieve their goals. They cannot wait. But higher wakefulness is not an achievement. It is a gift, a treasure beyond all achievements. Yet, it requires every bit or more of the discipline that achievement requires. Waiting for God means something unexpected, something that the world of competition and achievement cannot grasp. We must dispel the myths that the world of competition and achievement render about waiting so we can begin to comprehend waiting for God for what it really is.

Myth #1: Waiting is lonely

There is some truth to this statement. In our competitive world, the crowd rushes ahead, grasping for the cutting edge. Stay on top of the latest developments in cyberspace or the world will leave you behind. Keep up with fashion so you can dress for success. If you see an opening for a job with a higher salary, do not look over your shoulder at the co-workers you care about. Go for it.

The wise know that waiting in practical affairs may prove prudent more times than we realize. Nevertheless, our fear of being left behind makes us err more times than not toward stampeding with the herd. Those who choose to wait, therefore, often find themselves walking alone even if they walk down the right path.

Waiting is lonely when we see things from a competitive point of view, but not when we see things through the eyes of love. Paul cast a loving gaze toward the earth and wrote: "For the creation waits with eager longing for the revealing of the children of God; . . . and not only the creation, but we ourselves, who have the first fruits of the Spirit, groan inwardly while we wait for adoption, the redemption of our bodies" (Romans 8:19, 23). Through love we see our common task of waiting for God. Those "who have the first fruits of the Spirit" wait wakefully. They know that all the hurry to get ahead just distracts us from our deeper yearning for God, our waiting for God to make us whole.

We do not wait alone. We wait with the person in the next pew, the next door neighbor, the single mother in the trailer park on the other side of town, the starving child in Africa. We wait with the stone and the tree and, yes, the squirrel. We can have compassion for the squirrel because we share the common burden of waiting. Yet, we stand apart from the squirrel because we know for Whom we wait.

Myth #2: Waiting is punishment

In our culture, waiting very often takes on a negative meaning. When the doctor sees us an hour and a half after our appointment time, when traffic makes us a half hour late for work, when an inexperienced clerk delays the delivery of our package, we feel demeaned or robbed or both. When God bids us wait, we take it as punishment or worse, the caprice of an arrogant deity.

The view that waiting for God constitutes punishment finds support not only in our culture, but in scripture.

I am weary with my crying;
> my throat is parched.
My eyes grow dim
> with waiting for my God.

(Psalm 69:3)

The psalmist's agonized waiting results not only from feeling overwhelmed by life, but from a longing for God to draw near (v.18).

The Christian tradition maintains that because we separated ourselves from God by aspiring to be gods, a chasm yawns between God and us. Not only space fills the chasm, but time as well. We see God's face only when God crosses over. We know God only in God's time. Even then only the watchful see, the wakeful know. In his life, death, and resurrection, Jesus assured the chasm's closing, but only in God's time.

"In the beginning was the Word, and the Word was with God, and the Word was God. He was in the beginning with God. All things came into being through him, and without him, not one thing came into being" (John 1:1-3). Here is another song, only unlike the simple, sunny tones of the waiting psalmist or the springtime melody of the ravens, this song requires an entire symphony. It soars above time, and there it finds the carpenter's son from Galilee, creating the world.

Jesus came within time, but Jesus stands above time. Jesus died in six hours on a cross, but Jesus wove the fabric of each moment. And God said that it was good.

There is, therefore, a paradox in each tick of the clock. Each tick is a step toward the grave, a trace of corruption and decay. Yet, every instant is a wonderful creation, a sacrament, a container of treasures beyond our imagining. A caress soothes the sting of each moment we wait. "My soul waits for the LORD more than watchmen wait for the morning, more than watchmen wait for the morning," the psalmist sings, savoring each tick of the clock.

Those who wait watchfully know that each tick of the clock brings us closer to death, yes, but closer to home also. So waiting is sweet, and more than that, waiting is nourishment for the journey. In the gift of each moment, the Word wove more causes for joy than we can fathom. To prepare us for the long haul, God gave us the blessing of moments and days.

Thus, waiting for God is not punishment in the final analysis, but joy. We wait with serenity rather than anguish when we focus our gaze on the day or even the moment rather than the distant future. The alcoholic recovers "one day at a time," and in the day, God provides countless blessings even amid suffering. "So do not worry about tomorrow, for tomorrow will bring worries of its own," Jesus taught after praising the ravens and the lilies for trusting God to provide what they need one day at a time. "Today's trouble is enough for today" (Matthew 6:34), as is today's grace.

Myth #3: Waiting is escape

We abuse religion when we use it as a refuge from taking responsibility for our problems or for injustices in our social sphere. "The devil made me do it," quips the comedian, and we laugh to keep from crying. Someone lifts Jesus' words, "You always have the poor with you" (Mark 14:7), out of context as a justification for ignoring the immense problem of poverty. All too many nod their heads. The rest look the other way.

Such excuses for inaction may help us wait for the idiot to wise up or the wretched of the earth to go away, but they do not help us wait for God. In our waiting for the face of God, we first found it on the face of a suffering Christ, and we still find it amid the hungry, thirsty, lonely, naked, sick, and imprisoned (Matthew 25:31-46). If we seek God's face with half an ounce of common sense, we will respond to God's suffering with acts of compassion, not waiting around.

Nevertheless, waiting for God has a cautious dimension too. Watchfulness does not mix well with impulsive rushing to fix this problem or that. Waiting for God does not fit the profile of the in-your-face activist who harasses the clientele at abortion clinics or who condescendingly corrects a co-worker's politically incorrect phrases. Waiting for God is not self-righteous, not so assured of God's will that it tramples those who stand in the way. One who waits for God waits for God's will. This takes the hard work of discernment along with an attitude of humility.

Those who wait for God know that they wait for One whose thoughts are not our thoughts and whose ways are not our ways, whose mind soars higher above us than the stars (Isaiah 55:8-9). Jesus compared the Holy Spirit to the wind which "blows where it chooses, and you hear the sound of it, but you do not know where it comes from or where it goes" (John 3:8). Those who wait for God know that in the presence of such divine thoughts and such perfect freedom, we are dust.

We do not wait for perfect knowledge of God's will, or else we would never act. On the same token, we must never wait until our souls are completely pure before deciding that we qualify for decisive action in God's name. Yet, we must listen to God day by day. We must keep an ear open to our neighbor, an ear to our hearts, and a third ear to God. Faith is a journey led by God. We pause, wait, and listen for the Guide who speaks more often than not in a still, small voice that requires careful, patient attention. Those who wait for God anticipate God's action without retreating into inaction.

However, when we take action without waiting at all, we too often do so to escape reality more so than we would by waiting. The impulsive spender escapes into the fine clothes on the rack. The pushy father, fleeing his own sense of inadequacy, presses his son to Little League stardom rather than giving him time to be a child. The young man who will not wait for intimacy tries to force sex on his date, making himself a rapist and her a victim.

Most good things in life require waiting. God called the creation good then took a day to let it all sink in. The best things will take a lifetime to ripen.

Moreover, if one lives as if waiting for God is an escape from reality, one implies that God does not exist. Of course, the atheist must conclude that those who wait for God wait foolishly for a dream. Yet, all too many of us who call ourselves Christians postpone waiting for God as if we escape reality by doing otherwise. We try to manage our world, wringing our hands when we cannot grasp control of our workplaces or churches or our teenage daughters' sullen thoughts. Thus, we live as if our destinies rest in human hands, not God's hands.

Amid adversity, waiting for God boldly testifies to God's reality. When Jesus taught his disciples to turn the other cheek and cautioned us to expect persecution, he prepared them to wait for God. Such waiting is not escape. It is more realistic than our macho culture that bids us strike first lest we be struck. Waiting for God trusts in God's power rather than our own, and Christ's conquest of death attests to the fact that even God's weakness overcomes any human strength.

This chapter reveals much of what waiting for God is not: It is not lonely. We wait with all of creation. It is not punishment. By waiting for God one day at a time, we find serenity. It is not an escape from reality. Waiting for God requires that we respond to suffering while at the same time accepting the reality that God will redeem us in God's time.

In a word, waiting for God is not passive, but active. It is not bland but creative. Living spiritually in the real world means waiting for God creatively in everything we do. Having discussed what waiting for God is not, we turn in the next chapter to further define what creative waiting for God is.

QUESTIONS FOR REFLECTION AND DISCUSSION

1. Over the course of our lives, we come to many crossroads at which we must choose between

waiting and taking immediate action. This occurs at crucial times such as choosing a mate or a new job, and it also occurs in more mundane situations such as deciding whether to make a purchase now or wait until the prices drop. Remember a time when you chose to wait and decided you were glad that you did. How do you see God's hand at work in your decision and in your waiting?

2. Which myth do you find most challenging? (1) Waiting is lonely. (2) Waiting is punishment. (3) Waiting is escape. Select a biblical passage from those quoted in this chapter or any other passage that challenges your assumptions about waiting for God. Meditate prayerfully on the passage, and ask God to shape you with it. Write down what God reveals.

3. Much of our culture has little tolerance for waiting, as exemplified in the statement, "Few remember a world in which everything depended on rains that fall when they fall, on letting the watermelon take its sweet time to ripen, on the wisdom of old age." If we think of the church as the conscience of the culture, how should the church address this situation?

CHAPTER 6

Creative and Free

MOMENTS IN A COSMIC DRAMA

After watching a good movie, I suffer from a temporary depression that I call "post-cinematic blues." It derives from the feeling that my life is not half as interesting as the lives of the movie's main characters. Perhaps if I approached life less cautiously, I would find myself in the middle of a highly intriguing case of espionage. Had I pursued a career in the Air Force or in engineering, perhaps I would stand a chance to serve on the crew of the starship *Enterprise*. My decisions to forego the driven pursuit of wealth and power lower the odds that my victories and tragedies will capture the imagination of Hollywood producers.

To cope with this syndrome, I remind myself that everyone's life, including mine, includes the stuff of good movies. Movies give us poignant scenes that add up to a couple of hours; yet, these scenes may tell a story set in a time span of days, months, years, decades, or sometimes centuries. They create the illusion of lives filled with drama and irony, lacking mundane moments or hum-drum days. Mediocre movies edit out the everyday. Better movies include occasional quiet moments on lazy Sundays or the drudgery of work at the mill, but even those scenes foreshadow the big event to come.

With the help of a screenwriter or psychotherapist, people can edit their lives down to two hours that capture the uniqueness of their character, the tragedy or joy of their destiny, the critical event when their heroic side shone through. But in the cosmic drama of God's coming, every moment counts. Every moment points to the culmination of history, when the kingdom of God comes out of the cracks and crevices and back alleys, when the face of God in suffering people becomes a face of joy.

How we wait for God comes down to how we face those moments. In the last chapter, we discussed how waiting for God differs from what our culture would have us think about waiting. Rather than allowing the world to leave us behind, those who wait keep intimate company with all of creation. Rather than suffering unmitigated agony until the wait ends, those who wait taste the sweetness of each day. Rather than escaping reality, those who wait participate boldly in the reality of God. In this chapter, we will gain an appreciation of the creativity of waiting for God, and in the second part of this book, we will explore and celebrate that creative waiting in specific dimensions of our daily lives.

THE WEIGHT OF FREEDOM

An NBC interviewer once asked Rabbi Abraham Joshua Heschel, "What message have you for young people?" Heschel responded, ". . . Let them remember that there is meaning beyond absurdity. Let them be sure that every deed counts, that every word has power, and that we all can do our share to redeem the world in spite of all absurdities and all frustrations and all disappointments.

"And above all, [let them] remember . . . to build a life as if it were a work of art."[1]

An artist stands before a blank canvas. A poet hunches over a blank page. A sculptor contemplates a block of granite. A composer sits at a piano in silence. I awaken and face 1440 unfilled minutes of a day that has never been and that will never be again.

The truly wakeful face those minutes as an artist. The artist faces blankness and feels freedom, freedom to paint new lines and colors, to issue words that take on a life of their own, to form a strong woman from the rock, to make a melody as new as the morning light and as old as the sun. The wakeful one faces the day with similar promise, to fill the moments with a meaning beyond absurdity, with deeds that count, with words that open eyes.

The artist must have faith. With every brush stroke, with every word, with every blow of the chisel, with every note, the artist lets go. The color, the verse, the shape, the sound all take on their own life. The disciplined and skilled artist will attend like a midwife to the new life that emerges. The artist trusts the mystery of creative powers beyond comprehension for guidance.

Since my life is a work of art, I too must have faith to face each day. I plunge a flawed self into a frustrating world with hope that God will take whatever I make of my day and use it toward redeeming the world. I do deeds. I speak words. I listen. I touch. I pray. I trust the mystery of God's incomprehensible powers for guidance—and for more than guidance. For the redemption of the world.

The empty canvas, the blank page, the unformed stone, and the silence all form fields of freedom in which the artist can play. So it is with the days of the wakeful. Yet, freedom offers more than the light, airy opportunity to play. Freedom also offers the burdensome weight of responsibility. When I can fill the nothingness before me with countless hues or meanings or forms or sounds, I must take a leap of faith or the infinite possibilities will crush me.

Existentialist thinkers from Soren Kierkegaard to Jean-Paul Sartre and from Fyodor Dostoevsky to Albert Camus exposed the terrible burden of freedom. Americans have a national holiday to celebrate freedom, and so we should. But let us not fool ourselves into thinking that freedom is a day off to shoot fireworks, drink beer, and watch baseball. Freedom is a blank canvas and the responsibility to paint something that reveals more than canvas and paint. Freedom is 1440 blank minutes and the responsibility to fill them with a life that reveals God.

We celebrate freedom—but only the freedom we can bear. Most of us know places to hide from freedom. We hide in a bottle, in the glow of the TV tube, in the pursuit of thinness, in an affair, or in a fantasy. Most of us, most of the time, run from freedom like a squirrel running from lightning.[2]

We celebrate the freedom from interference with our right to do what we please. We toast our precious license. Yet, the freedom to tackle the creative task of living a meaningful life scares us to death.

None of us has perfect freedom, of course, and some of us have less than others. Yet, no one has so little freedom that Heschel's call "to build a life as if it were a work of art" is canceled. Even the lonely man in the hospital room staring at stumps where once there were legs has choices about how to carry himself, how to interpret his limitations, what kind of disposition to offer to the world. Even the poor woman in China who lacks a voice in society because of ancient cultural bigotries and new state despotism can live a life that sings with faith that God will give someone ears to hear her spirit's song.

Freedom is as light as a flying ballerina. God gave it to Adam and Eve in the garden to enjoy along with all the other sweet fruits and fragrant flowers. Freedom is as heavy as a lead weight. It led to the Fall, and God let Adam and Eve take it with them like a ball and chain.

Why do we still wait for God? Perhaps because God waits for us. Perhaps God waits for us to fully use the freedom God gave us. Perhaps, from God's perspective, we have not begun to use our freedom.

Such speculation aside, we know this much. We wait for God, and each waiting moment offers a terrible gift of freedom. Whether freedom becomes a blessing or a burden in the interim depends on how creatively we live our moments.

BACK TO THE THEATER

Let's take a second look at my post-cinematic blues. After a couple of hours of watching a seemingly normal guy like me rise from rags to riches, save the planet from hostile space aliens, or otherwise win the adoration of everyone in the theater, I wonder if I took a wrong turn somewhere on the road of life. Maybe I've done okay. I may have a family and a house and a good job and a decent investment portfolio. Perhaps I even did one or two things better than average. But who would write a movie script about this life?

A wise therapist tells me that someone already wrote the script. It is called "Mid-Life Crisis," and it stars everyone my age in the western world. Somehow I do not think that movie will make me feel better.

At the squirrel level or lowest level of wakefulness, I may do one of two things. I may scramble to make my life interesting, but it usually does not measure up to the movies. I may escape into a long weekend of watching other guys play football on the tube, but that only compounds the problem. At the lowest level, I live the rest of my life in a mediocre struggle against mediocrity.

At the citizen level, I step outside of myself. I realize that the stories of those around me matter, and I find that by listening to their stories and loving them, my story becomes more interesting. Yet, I find myself vacillating between giving and taking. I try to give enough but not too much lest I deplete my supply of love and sink back to the squirrel level, desperate to take care of myself. I try to write my own story while caring about the stories of others.

This freedom to write my life story will torment me until I learn what the sculptor knows. Sculptors eye a slab of marble and see a figure already there. Then they chip off the excess granite and a work of art emerges. The sculptor does not create the figure. The sculptor sets it free. Other artists, including those who write stories, report a similar process. The work of art seems to already be "out there," and the artist's craft only reveals it.

When Rabbi Heschel advised the young to live their lives as if they were works of art, I do not think he meant for them to force their lives into a mold or make their stories conform to a preconceived plot. I think he meant for them to wait watchfully for God to reveal their stories. Then they must set their stories free. This requires freely chosen faithfulness to the God who lovingly shapes their lives.

Higher wakefulness faces each day with the confidence that this day will be another word in the story God gives us. The day waits for me to create something, but not a portrait of myself, a poem that gives voice to my spirit, a bust of my head, or a ballad in memory of me. Today I must heed the call to creatively set free God's story of my life. I cannot do that by looking in the mirror. I can only do that by looking at God, seeking God's face, hearing and telling God's own story. Then I will see the figure in the stone. Then I can begin to chisel it out with my choices and my deeds. Nothing Hollywood produces has a prayer to match the stories God gives us.

Waiting for God ultimately beats the post-cinematic blues or mid-life crises or any other neurotic entanglements we might create for ourselves in our quest for self-fulfillment. Waiting for God means playing in a more compelling drama than our own.

It means playing in God's drama and freely following God's lead.

THE DETAILS

If every moment counts in God's drama, if the divine One creatively and lovingly writes out my story moment by moment, if every instant of my life is a blank canvas awaiting my brush stroke, why do I have a stack of dishes to wash? Why do I have income tax forms to fill out? Why do I referee children's fights over who gets to play what video game when? Why must I field daily phone calls from telemarketers reading their scripts about time shares and long-distance calling plans and carpet cleaning services?

Strange as it may seem, those may be the most crucial details to which we attend on a given day. Each tempts us with a pride that says we are too good to bother. Each offers the opportunity to step for a moment into God's house. With infinite love and attention, God offers to us these seemingly insignificant moments as opportunities for holiness. Jesus taught that how we attend to the details will determine whether we attend to him when he returns in a big way:

> Then the kingdom of heaven will be like this. Ten bridesmaids took their lamps and went to meet the bridegroom. Five of them were foolish, and five were wise. When the foolish took their lamps, they took no oil with them; but the wise took flasks of oil with their lamps. As the bridegroom was delayed, all of

them became drowsy and slept. But at midnight there was a shout, "Look! Here is the bridegroom! Come out to meet him." Then all those bridesmaids got up and trimmed their lamps. The foolish said to the wise, "Give us some of your oil, for our lamps are going out." But the wise replied, "No! there will not be enough for you and for us; you had better go to the dealers and buy some for yourselves." And while they went to buy it, the bridegroom came, and those who were ready went with him into the wedding banquet; and the door was shut. Later the other bridesmaids came also, saying, "Lord, lord, open to us." But he replied, "Truly I tell you, I do not know you." Keep awake therefore, for you know neither the day nor the hour.

(Matthew 25:1-13)

Attention to the detail of having sufficient oil for their lamps prepared some to celebrate with the bridegroom. Their wakefulness enabled them to attend to the necessary details. This even freed them to sleep, and when they awakened, they were ready.

So it is with the dishes, the taxes, the way we keep peace and order in our homes, and the way we entertain telemarketing strangers. Each seemingly insignificant task presents an opportunity to prepare for the bridegroom. How we approach the details trains us to recognize the face of God.

Only God will ultimately open our eyes and awaken us because sin distorts our perception and confounds our actions. Thus, chapter 4 discussed our need to repent, literally turn around and offer our whole selves for God to renew. Just seeing and doing according to instructions will not awaken us to God. We must rely on God and approach each task awaiting the grace God offers in it. Each task becomes a discipline that conditions us to wait for God.

This implies that the wakeful do not put religion in a compartment. Religion does not grow in a pot of its own on a shelf alongside our career pot, domestic pot, financial pot, leisure pot, social pot, or political pot. Religion spills into every pot like water nourishing all that grows there. Thus, the wakeful attend to all aspects and details of life from the perspective of faith in the one God who both guides the nations and numbers the hairs on our heads.

QUESTIONS FOR REFLECTION AND DISCUSSION

1. If a Hollywood producer finally discovered you and made a movie about your life, what should the title be? What two or three scenes would be most critical? What would the movie reveal about God?

2. Think of someone whom you believe has followed Rabbi Heschel's advice "to build a life as if it were a work of art." What do you observe about the way this person lives that brings him or her to mind?

3. What daily activity seems most like meaningless drudgery to you? Devise one or more possible

answers to the question, Why did God give me this task to do? Use prayer, meditation, reading from the Bible, or conversation with creative people whom you trust to help you.

PART II

The Details
of the Day

CHAPTER 7

celebrating the Day

THE GOD OF CHAOS AND ORDER

I awaken before the alarm. My stomach aches softly for food. Thoughts about today's tasks rush in as if they waited in the darkness all night long for my eyes to open. I try to shoo them away, but like cats at feeding time, they find their way back. Perhaps if I empty my mind, my hunger will fade. My stomach gnaws. The digital clock brands the darkness with the time: 5:34. With all hope of sleep lost, I lie there wondering what I'm waiting for.

The day ahead is Tuesday. The off-beat rhythm of the weekend now forgotten, Tuesday holds a bit of everything: work and play, sacred and profane, solitude and community. How I live Tuesday is how I live my life.

The thoughts of the day that sabotage my slumber offer nothing remarkable. A phone call to return. Clients in my counseling practice returning to the harbor of my office after a week's voyage. A meeting with my staff. Another meeting with my boss. Interruptions. A towering stack of mail.

Thoughts of work awaken me because work pumps my adrenaline. Home pumps my heart. My wife—a more gifted sleeper than I—breathes long and deep at my side. Plans and projects always clamor for our attention. The house needs new carpet. The hedges need clipping. What will we do for supper? What will we do with our stress when we both get home from work?

These thoughts carry me from sleep to wakening. Yet, I lie a little longer in the warmth of the bed, the depth of the darkness, the peace of the silence. I wonder how to take the warmth, depth, and peace with me through the day.

I see the day ahead through bifocals. Through one lens, I see chaos. I hear phones ringing, my name called, the sound of a client sobbing. Faces pitch before me as on the deck of a ship in a storm. Somebody says something about suicide. A client digs in his heels against the changes he says he wants to make. A co-worker seems unexplainably angry. When the lines are not busy, I get answering machines when I call. I receive a cryptic memo. A cat throws up. My wife has a bad day at work and brings it home.

> Come and see the works of the LORD,
> the desolations he has brought on the earth.
> . . . .
> "Be still, and know that I am God."
>
> (Psalm 46:8,10, NIV)

God is somehow in the chaos and above it. The wind of the Spirit blows where it will. God calls from the storm, "Be still."

Through another lens, I see the same day and find order. Ritual gives the day rhythm. In a moment, the sun will rise and begin its trek across the heavens. I can see the faint glow of daybreak on the bedroom blinds. I kiss my wife's cheek, and she moans softly. As I touch my bare feet to the cold, hardwood floor, I turn off the alarm clock and plan to awaken her a little later. I slip on my bathrobe and turn on a small fan to drown out the sounds of floorboards creaking and faucets running as I start my morning ritual before she does. The dog stretches, and with a little prompting she accompanies me out the bedroom door that I close ever so gently.

Each day starts with the same ritual. Somehow the ritual makes room in my soul for the warmth and depth and silence to follow me from the cocoon of bed and bedroom into the chaos of the day.

This is the day that the LORD has made;
  let us rejoice and be glad in it.
                              (Psalm 118:24)

If I remember them, those words of the psalmist breathe holiness into the rituals of the morning.

"In the beginning when God created the heavens and the earth, the earth was a formless void and darkness covered the face of the deep, while a wind from God swept over the face of the waters" (Genesis 1:1-2). God sends a wild wind into the chaos of the day and gives the world shape and substance with a word. We move back and forth between chaos and order. For God, chaos and order are one. Both offer windows to the hearts of the beloved.

Mortals cannot grasp chaos and order at once as God can, so wakeful ones keep a sailor's eye to the wind, watching the signs of its shifts, its intensity, the weather it brings. They must direct their ships by the whims of the invisible wind and the deep, dark tide. This is how they find God through the chaos of the day.

Yet, they must also listen for the word and dance to its song. They must live in the order that God brings to chaos, and they do so in ritual. Thus, ritual and word shape the worship of the wakeful, and the wakeful find in the rituals of any typical weekday cause to celebrate the creative love of God. In the rituals of waking, eating, loving, working, and maintaining a household, a typical day becomes a day of worship.

THE RITUALS

The morning then follows a series of rituals from feeding the animals to feeding myself, from checking the weather to getting dressed, from calisthenics to taking the dog out, from greeting my wife with a hug and a kiss to watching a few minutes of cold, hard news on TV. I shave and brush my teeth. My wife and I dash around semi-madly as the time to leave approaches, dodging each other, sharing reminders of errands and phone calls. I pack my lunch. If all goes well, I squeeze in time for Bible reading, journaling, and prayer.

The day begins with multiple, elaborate rituals, and rituals can kill. Ritual can keep the body busy and hot while the heart goes numb and cold. Ritual can close us up in a sheltered world without the God who sends a divine wind into the chaos of our worlds. It can make us so insistent on order that we miss the spontaneity of living. When this happens, we speak of the routines of the morning as going through the motions, and we despair.

Yet, those who accept the rituals of the morning as gifts of God, as praise to the Lord of the new day will find wakefulness and spontaneity in ritual. Those who seek God-given meaning in common rituals will find uncommon holiness in each day. They will be ready when the bridegroom comes, when the wind of the Spirit shifts, when God creates something new.

Take for instance brushing our teeth: We all do it. It presents a rich opportunity to laugh at ourselves, our puffy eyes, our disheveled hair. For no particular reason, I do it in front of the mirror sometimes, and I walk aimlessly around the house at other times. We prepare ourselves to encounter others when we brush our teeth, and with our mouths filling with minty white foam, we prepare in humility. It is the humbling of the self before the kiss or the hello. We pay every person respect before we meet them, whitening our teeth, shielding our dragon breath.

It's hard to do anything else while brushing teeth. With one hand occupied, the other can do very little. Heaven help us if we try to talk. For those few moments, we set aside everything to prepare our mouths for the world. We are not judged clean or unclean by what we put into our mouths, but by what comes out, Jesus said. Yet, we can brush our teeth and pray (without moving our lips) that God will keep our mouths clean and offer through them words that create rather than destroy.

We are born in ritual, and we die in ritual. So it is with our days. I begin with rituals of preparation such as brushing my teeth and finish with rituals of closing. Evening rituals prepare us for sleep. Sleep is the ultimate ritual of faith: We let go of all our cares and defenses, recline in the darkness, and give up consciousness. I do not see how atheists or those who believe in a cruel God can make themselves so vulnerable and deny having even an iota of faith in unseen powers.

Such letting go requires for many of us a gradual process of bidding farewell to the day and entering the vulnerability and mystery of night. We talk over our day with spouse or friend, reveling in its small victories and bemoaning its small defeats. We prepare a final meal, eat it, and perhaps come back for a snack just before bed. We read or do crossword puzzles or listen to music to clear our heads of the day's residual static.

Our ritual takes on a rhythm, sharing memories of our day then withdrawing into the forgetfulness of sleep. Like inhaling and exhaling, we take in enough of our day to let it nourish us and let go of enough of our day to take what nourishment the rest and dreaming of night will bring. I shower at night, my way of letting go of the residue of the day, and I eat a snack as if building up strength for a journey. Each day, like all of life, also has a rhythm of birth and death, each stage and step marked by new life and losses. Exhale, inhale. Farewell, greetings. Die, live again.

The rhythms are holy; yet, we must not force holy meaning into them. In Jesus' time, the Pharisees forced holy meaning into the details of the day, separating music from rhythm. The rituals became wooden, burdensome. What one wore, how one drove the oxen, whether a man talked with a woman, the recipe for cakes all grew heavy with holiness in the Pharisees' system for attending to the details of the day.

Those who wait for God let God do the creating. They do not try to create the meaning in the rituals. Rather, they let the rituals unfold and reveal holiness. They listen to life.

Those who wait for God let rituals follow their daily repetitions, but they trust God to open their eyes to the newness of life through these repetitions. I once attended a Monet exhibit which consisted of nothing but paintings of bridges, often the same bridge, but never the same vision. The ingenious impressionist saw new patterns of light with each new day, new colors with each hour. Contemplating the same bridge for weeks and months, repeating the ritual of seeing and painting, Monet discovered something new each time and shared each new discovery with a grateful world.

"Remember . . . to build a life as if it were a work of art," the rabbi said to the youth of the world before his departure. Do not grow bored with your days, for that reflects a failure of wakefulness, wasting away with impatience. Do not seek to escape into new places and fantasies, but attend to the rituals that God gives you to enact with the sun that rises and walks the rim of the sky, with the night creatures waiting for nightfall to sing, with the stars swirling in their ageless pattern. You participate in creation's dance—and more. In your ritual, God creates new meaning, and you, unlike the sun or tree frog or constellation, have eyes to see it, ears to hear it, lips to pray it and share the wonder with the God who gave it. Wait with the faith of the artist to find it.

RITUALS SHARED

Each morning, my wife and I make up our bed together. The task has utilitarian purposes—to keep dust off the sheets and keep the cats from wallowing in them, leaving fur and who knows what else. It certainly serves an aesthetic purpose, laying out the flowery comforter and bringing order to the crumpled and twisted covers. Yet, it seems to me more of a way to commemorate the night. We made it through another night together. We prayed together in that bed, gave up all consciousness side by side. We held each other, perhaps made love, perhaps just drew peace from each other's warmth and casual touches and strokes. One may have awakened the other from a nightmare.

If one dreamed an especially vivid dream, the other did not know the drama, although it happened there in the same bed. We may talk about dreams while we make up the bed. We may cross that bridge of sharing our lives, or we may keep the moods and visions of the night to ourselves, sealing them under the sheets. We will return to that place, together and apart at once, facing the night together and alone in bed. We make up the bed, marking the transition from a night's journey to a mysterious day ahead, together and apart.

My wife especially needs to remake the bed at night. She wants the sheets lined up just so, and she wants them folded under our chins. I get in bed first and try to read while she fluffs the covers over my body and covers my book with the blanket. I tell her she's obsessive-compulsive. She tells me I'm lazy. We laugh, together and apart. She, the extrovert, marks the transition to night by attending to her environment—the bed. I, the introvert, mark the transition by attending to my soul. She joins me with a book.

We read our separate books, then join hands to pray. God is there in bed with us, so it's a wonder that we ever sleep. We pray a string of petitions, for healing of whatever may ail us or someone we love. We pray for the blessings of children, growing love, friends and family, and meaningful work. We ask for protection in the night, protection for everyone we care for, including pets. We put it all in the hands of the Spirit who hovers over the chaos of life like God's wind over a dark and watery planet. We put it all in the wind that blows where it will.

We turn out the light with a kiss before we pray. After the prayer, we tell each other that we love each other. Then we face the night together. Ritual seals love. It invites the God who is love into our lives and into the night with us.

> The Lord Jesus on the night when he was betrayed took a loaf of bread, and when he had given thanks, he broke it and said, "This is my body that is for you. Do this in remembrance of me." In the same way he took the

cup also, after supper, saying, "This cup is the
new covenant in my blood. Do this, as often as
you drink it, in remembrance of me." For as
often as you eat this bread and drink the cup,
you proclaim the Lord's death until he comes.
. . . So then, my brothers and sisters, when you
come together to eat, wait for one another.

(1 Corinthians 11:23-26,33)

With this ritual, Jesus sealed a life before submit-
ting in his passion to the night of sin and death. He
and his disciples were together, yet apart. They were
together in eating and drinking and making a
covenant to remember Jesus. They were apart in
their separate, bewildered expectations about the
night to come. Jesus sealed his life with a ritual of
love, a ritual shared with his friends, a ritual that still
gives meaning and love to our lives together as his
friends two millennia later.

The Lord's Supper, whether we celebrated it last
Sunday or more Sundays ago than we can recall,
leaves its mark on this day as we begin and end the
day. It leaves its mark on our eating and drinking
together, on our tidying the sheets together, our reading together, our sleeping together. Through it we
share our passage from day and into night and into
day again with Jesus. We share our passage from
moment to moment, from work to rest, from togeth-
erness to aloneness with Jesus and with the love for
one another that is Jesus' gift.

The Lord's Supper affects today's rituals, but not
necessarily through conscious recollection. Most of
us do not remember the Lord's Supper after Sunday

any more than we remember Sunday's shaving or applying make-up or feeding the dog. It affects weekdays, nevertheless, the way any note inserted into a song affects the entire melody. From the perspective of the one God who listens to the whole melody of our lives, it adds unmistakable beauty to each day.

All the rituals of Sunday affect weekdays this way—the rising and the singing of familiar hymns, the bowing our heads in silence, the responsive reading of psalms, the dropping of money into the brass plate, the repetition of the Lord's prayer, the Apostles' Creed, and the doxology. These rituals affect the whole music of our lives and lift the meaning of weekday rituals a little higher.

We may not remember these rituals as we share meals and greetings and housework through the week, but we remember the faces. We remember the older woman who rose with slow determination to sing the doxology two rows up. We remember the tall, thin young man who sang off key behind us. We remember the teenager who passed the collection plate down the aisle. We remember the prayer concerns, the stories shared in the halls and classrooms, the pains born and joys shared alone and together in church. It is not always intimate. Sometimes it is not even kind. But it is always love.

Without ritual, we mortals would not know what to do with love. How would we share our love as a community of believers without the rituals we share on Sunday morning? How would we share our love as a family on Tuesday without the rituals of rising and sleeping and everything else we do together in the rhythm of each day? "Do this in remembrance of me,"

Jesus said as he broke the bread and poured the wine, giving us a ritual context for sharing love on Sunday and everyday.

QUESTIONS FOR REFLECTION AND DISCUSSION

1. Several daily activities were discussed as rituals that disclose meaning. For instance, brushing one's teeth in the morning was presented as a way to begin the day by humbly honoring all who would come into contact with us that day. Consider another routine daily activity of your choice. What might it mean? What does that activity disclose about God's presence and work in your day?

2. For my wife and me, making up the bed together bears this resemblance to the ritual of the Lord's Supper: it helps us to celebrate our love. Consider another routine activity that you share with someone you love. How does it reveal your love? How can you remember Jesus with that ritual?

3. This chapter presented the rituals of corporate worship as enhancing the spiritual harmony of weekdays even if we do not consciously remember Sunday's worship. On any weekday, reflect upon one of the rituals of corporate worship that you find meaningful. Try to reenact that ritual. How does this chosen ritual reveal God's meaning and love for you on this day?

CHAPTER 8

Spiritual Exercises

This book focuses on the search for spiritual significance in ordinary life. Such a focus implicitly contrasts our ordinary days with extraordinary occasions. In the most extraordinary event Christians recall, Christ rose from the dead two thousand years ago. But what about today with its deaths and other irretrievable losses? What about our ordinary, humdrum, unmiraculous non-Easter days?

Rulers rise and fall throughout history—David, Caesar, Constantine, Lincoln, Lenin, and others. They shake our worlds, then they depart. What about us common folk with our faith tested each day by the revolutions and rules of our households? What about the holy history of our virtually anonymous lives, how God called us, blessed us, poured wrath on us, raised us from the dead?

On Sundays many of us go to church with its stained glass windows, its pews and high ceilings, its worship leaders in academic gowns, its symbols, its songs. This is a Sunday place, not a weekday place. This is an Easter place, not an everyday place. Does religion reside only here? What about my home, my office, the grocery store, the park, the street? Is Sunday the day of spiritual life? What about Tuesday?

God is the Lord of every day, the Creator and Redeemer of home, office, supermarket, and park. The oil slicks, exhaust fumes, sirens, and boom boxes of city streets do not deter God from walking there. The deadlines, ringing phones, complaints, layoffs, interruptions, and coffee cups of the office do not prevent God from doing miracles there. The television commercials, crying children, laundry, and cluttered closets of home do not keep God out. For those with eyes to see and ears to hear, God abides in all places, Easter in all days.

Sunday worship services do nothing if they do not prepare us to worship on Monday through Saturday. In Sunday worship we prepare ourselves to live our faith wakefully during the week to come. Similarly, on each day, the ritual of taking a few minutes to worship God helps in living the day wakefully with an eye for the kingdom. Just as Sunday worship adds a note that transforms the melody of the entire week, so a few minutes of devotional exercises set the spiritual tone for the day.

Spiritual exercises condition our eyes to see God's face and our ears to hear God's call in ordinary days. Sunday mornings in the sanitized environs of church make obvious that which the nooks and crannies of our days hide: The kingdom of God is among us. The face of God is before us. We come here to wait for the Lord. Yet, we need not wait for Sunday. With a Bible in our laps in the quiet of the morning, with a prayer on our lips in rush hour traffic, with the wisdom of God on our minds as we face the small challenges of the day, we develop eyes to see and ears to hear.

This chapter will focus on three possible components of daily spiritual ritual—Bible study, meditation, and prayer—and how they color our vision of the rest of the day.

BIBLE STUDY

The Bible, like the rising sun, brings light in its own time. We cannot force it to rise according to our schedule, our agenda. Yet, we can rely on it. It always comes, giving vision and life.

We bring many agendas to the Bible. Some readers seek the rules by which to govern their lives and judge the lifestyles of others. Such folks place the Ten Commandments at the heart of scripture and see the rest of the Bible as commentary on it. The Bible serves as their blueprint for living or a road map to heaven.

Others see the Bible as a crystal ball into the future or a key to unlocking the nature of things. Extreme adherents to this agenda tease out the details of Revelation to predict the end of history or gather natural data to support one or both creation stories in Genesis. Other less extreme readers may find in the Bible a wellspring of insight into the human spirit wrestling with the Spirit of God.

Scholarly readers try to piece together a more accurate rendering of the historical course of ancient Israel and early Christianity. Or they critique the Bible as literature alongside all great literature. God and humankind become characters in a drama, and the truth of scripture becomes a truth much like that of *Moby Dick, Don Quixote*, or *The Scarlet Letter*.

All of these agendas have their merits and limitations. The faithful reader does well to listen to adherents of each program. Evaluating one's own behavior according to biblical principles, reading the newspaper with the eyes of an Old Testament prophet, or absorbing the tragedies and triumphs of King David can deeply enrich one's perspective. Yet, when we open the Bible and face the ancient text, the Holy Spirit hears the cry of our hearts longing to see and hear more clearly as disciples of Jesus. The Holy Spirit sets a higher agenda.

In his book, *Shaped by the Word*, Robert Mulholland distinguishes between the *informational* and *formational* approaches to scripture.[1] The agendas mentioned above take an informative approach: They seek certain kinds of information or insight. The reader implicitly approaches the Bible with the question, "What can I get from scripture today?"

The formational approach asks, "How will God shape me through the scripture today?" As a formative reader, I let scripture set the agenda and take the risk of trusting the Holy Spirit to make me new on God's terms, not on my terms. This does not mean taking the black and white text as my "command for the day." That is an informational approach. Rather, it means letting the Word sink in, facing honestly the feelings that the Word stirs in me, and dancing or struggling or resting with God in an active, personal relationship that will never let me be quite the same again.

Living relationships always sharpen vision. My wife, although beautiful to others, possesses a special beauty to me that years of sharing good days and bad days help me to see. Loving her changes me and sharpens my vision. I see her touch in the details of my life that I would not see without knowing her.

A relationship with God shared intimately in scripture transforms us and clarifies our vision all the more. *God* addresses us *through* the Bible. The book does not suffice in itself. If it did, then the story of David and Bathsheba would only tell us about another king who let an inflated ego smother his character. God uses David's sin to address all time. God addresses uniquely every heart that opens to the Spirit in reading that sordid story. David's sin is my sin, Uriah's death my death, Bathsheba's tragedy my tragedy as God draws me into the story and convicts me, wounds me, and loves me there. I will never be the same if I read it with faith.

One may read the Bible alone in the privacy of a study, but one never really reads it privately. The Bible draws me spiritually into the community of faith. It is literally the church's book, written for the community of faith, and selected by it. Moreover, to read the Bible formatively draws me into the faith of its characters and writers, into a community ancient and new.

That community and I, the reader, share common sinfulness, ignorance, and mortality. We are fallen creatures with inadequate words. So the Bible, written and read by imperfect people of faltering faith, might seem no more suited to convey God's word than a good novel or a walk in the woods. But when

I read it faithfully, a miracle takes place. God transforms that ancient and new community. God reaches back over the millennia and transforms the prophets and warriors and tax collectors and widows of the biblical era. God reaches down in the moment of my reading and changes me, opening my eyes.

Karl Barth offered a useful analogy to help us understand how the Bible helps us to see. He likened reading the Bible's ancient text to looking out a window.[2] Imagine that you stand at a window in your home and see a crowd of people looking up into the sky. What they see stirs some, disturbs others, entrances all. Many talk with each other with great animation. Some fall to their knees.

From this particular window, you cannot see the sky, at least not the part they watch so intently. But you can see the people's response. You begin to share the excitement and the wonder. You see more evidence of this source of wonder in the way the light plays on the treetops or in the sound of night creatures as the light fades. You may never see it directly but you might as well have because all the evidence of this mystery surrounds you, and you become a witness to it. It changes you.

After a while, you venture outside, looking up and about. For those still inside looking out, you become part of the strange and wonderful drama outside. Some of them join you.

The Bible reveals God not through dictation of perfect words for us to catalog and cite like a body of research to prove a point. The Bible reveals God through the union of imperfect people drawn to their Lord.

God reveals divine power through the weakness of the Bible's writers, its main characters, and its readers. God reveals holy truth through the love that draws them together across streets and nationalities and eons. The human hands that wrote the Bible reveal God far more richly than a dictation from heaven. The human characters in the drama disclose God far more decisively than a flawless syllogism. Such revelations would lead us to worship the words of the Bible or the logic of the theologians rather than God.

The few minutes you take in the morning or evening to read the Bible bring a quiet miracle into the day. It answers solitude with a cloud of witnesses, and if you read it with others, all the better. It interrupts the daily routine with a burning bush. In the quiet of the morning, God's messenger will bid you go serve the Lord. In the din of the day, Jesus will beckon, "Follow me." In time you see someone watching as if you are a kind of Bible yourself, a kind of unexpected revelation. Little by little, word by word, you will change. You will never be the same. You will never see the same.

MEDITATION

Everyone must find a routine for spiritual exercises that works for them. It takes time, trial and error, and prayer. The Spirit works it out with us. Some persons spend hours a day in prayer and meditation. Others keep extensive journals, cataloging all their feelings and insights. Some include song and sacrifice. Some get on their knees while others recline in a chair. Many pray in small doses in a few quiet morning moments, in the car on the way to work, while running, or while playing a musical instrument.

My morning routine typically begins with a Bible reading that follows the lectionary, a brief time of meditation, and then prayer. It takes thirty minutes, give or take a few. I do this most days, but not every day. A daily requirement becomes a daily chore or a daily reason to resent interruptions. God usually sends the interruptions, so I do not let my devotional time defeat itself by closing God out. Still I protect that time within reason, and my wife and I respect each other's sacred time.

For some a daily devotional time may be necessary, at least at first. It helps to develop the expectation. After a time of doing it habitually, one finds a deepening joy in these hours with God. Now that I have dropped the expectation that I must do it each morning, I delight in opportunities that I make or that God provides for my devotional exercises. Most days I find that the gift of time for spiritual exercises arrives. This works for me, at least for now.

The Bible reading—usually selected from that week's menu from the Revised Common Lectionary—opens my eyes and orients me. I find a verse or phrase or theme or image, and I chew on it for a while. I let it address my life at the time, and somehow the Bible always manages to do that. If I feel swamped at work, a psalm of pure praise reveals my workaholic tunnel vision, and I reorient my sights to the wideness of God. If I feel that my faith is weak, "Blessed are the poor in spirit," or the parable of the mustard seed remind me of God's great promise for small things like my faith. If I feel joy, the Bible completes my joy. If I feel pain, the Bible refuses to offer sugar and offers salve instead. The Bible and my life meet in ways as unique and diverse as the days themselves.

Meditation is what I do with that biblical focus between the reading and the praying. Some devotional books offer excellent excerpts from great spiritual writers on themes found in the scripture.[3] Their insights may enrich our interpretation of the scripture and of our lives, so such readings may help with meditation. I prefer, however, to write a short paragraph, nothing fancy. Writing helps me to integrate things. Bible study wakes me up and gives me a focus. Meditation enables me to put things together before I pray.

I do not always succeed. Sometimes I must wait for prayer before things come together in God's hands. At those times meditation at least enables me to open my heart, to prepare myself to listen to God in prayer. If all I have to offer in prayer is my confusion, God will sift out nuggets from my words or from my silence that I cannot find. At times, God may not show me those nuggets until much later after I forget this moment of prayer.

Meditation prepares me for the bridegroom. It is trimming the lamp of my soul, putting my inner house in order. I collect myself. I make myself presentable.

In transcendental meditation, one focuses on a flame or a word or a nonsense syllable until the mind blocks out everything else. A Buddhist monk in the lotus position repeating a mantra until his pulse practically ceases takes meditation to its athletic extreme. Psychologists and Christian contemplatives find that we have much to learn from them. But one need not sail for speed to enjoy sailing. One need not run for the prize to gain from running. The point is not to become a great meditator. The point is to do just enough to prepare for the bridegroom, then forget it. Focus on the bridegroom. Celebrate his joy.

For me this means reflecting on the brief scripture reading. I scribble a few thoughts on how one verse ties to another, how one theme ties to my concerns, how one chance phrase ties to mystery. Perhaps I choose a phrase and roll it around on my tongue for a while. I tie together loose ends, and that is preparation enough. I look up to meet the Son.

Prayer

Prayer is looking up to meet the Son. When friend meets friend on the street, some rituals help us to know what to do with the love. We shake hands, perhaps exchange a favorite phrase like, "Speak of the devil," or, "Well, look what the cat dragged in." We find something in the moment or in our shared memory to laugh or tease about. Or if we are a little more secure, we say what we really mean like, "Well how wonderful to see you, my friend. I hope you are well."

Such rituals help us to see each other, to forget ourselves and prepare for the unscripted, unexpected way that the conversation will unfold. Of course, with old friends, surprises are few, or at least less dramatic and more subtle. We share our news and open our ears to listen.

So it is with prayer. Bible reading and meditation are the greeting and the handshake. They orient us, help us focus and forget ourselves. Then we encounter the Son who meets us in human form, the Spirit who moves unexpectedly, the God who searches us and knows us. That encounter is prayer. It has no formula, no right or wrong way to do it.

In prayer we encounter a friend, so we can simply be ourselves, trusting God as a friend to handle our awkwardness gently, our rough edges and ill-chosen words mercifully. Yet, God is much more than a friend. If we think of God as no more than a friend, God becomes a reflection of ourselves, someone like us who shares our tastes and biases. Prayer becomes a conversation not with God, but with ourselves.

God is friendly, but more than a friend. God is close like a friend, but also closer than a friend. Psalm 139 offers a prayer that seeks to understand the closeness of God, and it concludes in awestruck unknowing:

> O LORD, you have searched me
>   and known me.
> You know when I sit down and
>   when I rise up;
>   you discern my thoughts from
>   far away.
> You search out my path and my
>   lying down,
>   and are acquainted with all
>   my ways.
> Even before a word is on my
>   tongue,

O LORD, you know it
    completely.
You hem me in, behind and
    before,
    and lay your hand upon me.
Such knowledge is too wonderful
    for me;
    it is so high that I cannot
    attain it.
How weighty to me are your
    thoughts, O God!
How vast is the sum of them!
    I try to count them—they are
    more than the sand;
I come to the end—I am still
    with you.

(Psalm 1-6, 17-18)

God's closeness mystifies the psalmist as much as God's distance and hiddenness. When we come before God in prayer, it behooves us to come with a dose of fear and trembling and a larger dose of gratitude that this One who made us and knows us and guides our lives chooses also to love us, to hear our prayers with friendliness.

It behooves us even more to listen. God speaks, though few of us hear God in the same audible way that we hear each other. The heart hears God. The heart offers its longings and has ears to hear in the silence or the wind or the groaning of the earth:

We know that the whole creation has been groaning in labor pains until now; and not only the creation, but we ourselves, who have the first fruits of the Spirit, groan inwardly while we wait for adoption, the redemption of our bodies.

(Romans 8:22-23)

And it is not only the heart that speaks and listens when we pray:

Likewise the Spirit helps us in our weakness; for we do not know how to pray as we ought, but that very Spirit intercedes with sighs too deep for words. And God, who searches the heart, knows what is the mind of the Spirit, because the Spirit intercedes for the saints according to the will of God.

(Romans 8:26-27)

We can pray freely because we do not pray alone. The Holy Spirit breathes prayer into us, even if we can find no words, even if the weight of life gags us. We can trust our heart's hearing in ·the silence because God searches our hearts and gives us discernment, a sense of God's mind at work. Those who participate in this quiet miracle of prayer may not always trust themselves to pray as they ought, but they can trust God to draw them near.

If wants clutter the mind, offer them up. If emotions stir and confuse, add them to the chorus of creation's groaning anticipation. If unbelief and boredom seep in, cry out, "I believe; help my unbelief!" (Mark 9:24). Then wait for a miracle. It will come.

Prayer brings miracles into the ordinary details of the day like an ink drop in a clear pitcher of water.

The ink spreads, tinting the water faint blue. Another drop tomorrow makes the water imperceptibly bluer. A drop each day eventually fills the pitcher with deep blue water, seemingly all ink.

So it is with prayer. One prayer colors the day with a barely visible hint of miracle. Daily prayer brings the miracles out into bolder relief after a while, and the signs of the kingdom in the hidden places become more apparent. A life of prayer is a miracle itself, deep with color, staining everything with the brilliance of God.

QUESTIONS FOR REFLECTION AND DISCUSSION

1. Read Psalm 139. Take a few minutes on each of several days over the next week to spend with that psalm. On each occasion, select a key word, phrase, or verse that addresses your current life in a unique way. Meditate on your selection by writing notes, reflecting, or just repeating it to yourself. Then pray. How did the reading and meditation affect your prayer? Do you find a different ritual more helpful? If so, what do you do, and how does it help you pray?

   Discuss this with someone in your church whose spiritual life inspires you.

2. Here is the Lord's Prayer broken down into seven short prayers:
   a) Our Father who art in heaven, hallowed be Thy name.
   b) Thy kingdom come.
   c) Thy will be done, on earth as it is in heaven.

d) Give us this day our daily bread.

e) Forgive us our debts as we forgive our debtors.

f) Lead us not into temptation, but deliver us from evil.

g) Thine is the kingdom, and the power, and the glory forever.

Pray and meditate on one of these each day this week. What do you learn about God? About yourself? About the Lord's Prayer? How does this exercise affect you when you pray it with the congregation on Sunday?

3. After several days of doing #1 and #2 above, take a moment at the end of the day to reflect on how they affected the other activities of your day. The effects may be profound or barely perceptible, but in either case they are important. What did you discover about God's influence on your daily activities?

CHAPTER 9

Meaningful work

A DESCENDANT OF BROTHER LAWRENCE

Recently, my wife and I decided to have central air conditioning installed in our home. Soon strangers inhabited our basement, carving out holes, routing ducts, and attaching a machine that looked like a UFO in the side yard. These strangers also roamed about in our living quarters, carving out more holes in the walls and the floor, installing grates and filters and a thermostat. One of our cats hid for days.

On the second day of the job, I came home for lunch. With tools scattered on the floor about him, a young man on his hands and knees stuck his head into the guest room closet and sawed a hole in the floor. I had not met him yet, but I knew that his co-worker in the basement below seemed rather gruff. So I expected the same of the young man. I needed to get something out of the closet, so I said, "Excuse me," as clearly and politely as I could since he held an electric saw in his hand.

My prejudice about him proved unfounded. He apologized unnecessarily for blocking my path and rose to face me. He wore a sweaty white tee-shirt and jeans over a lean, muscular frame. His intense but cheerful blue eyes and mussed up short brown hair gave him the look of a young man on an adventure. I suspected that every step along the way in this air-conditioning installation presented a new challenge that he eagerly embraced.

We quickly struck up a conversation. He said his name was Tim and that I looked familiar. We never figured out where he saw me before, but since he had lived in the area for all of his twenty-one years and I had lived there for ten at the time, we decided that he must have seen me on the street a few times. He did not attend the college where I worked.

Then Tim told me more about himself in a few short sentences than most of us can muster in the first five minutes with a new acquaintance: "I am the youth minister at Northside Church"—a new evangelical congregation that recently moved from a rented space in a shopping center to its own building. Then he added, "But somehow God gives me more of a ministry while I'm installing air conditioners than I get at church. It's not what I expected, but it's true."

I told him that I appreciated both his badly needed service to youth and the long-anticipated cool air. As he strapped his goggles back in place, he concluded, "Well, this job has the added benefit of keeping me humble." I appreciated humility in a man standing in my guest room holding an electric saw with a long, jagged blade.

Tim is a spiritual descendant of Brother Lawrence of the Resurrection, a monk in Paris who died over three hundred years before my conversation with Tim. Brother Lawrence spent most of his life working in the monastery kitchen. He also spent a few years making and repairing shoes for his brothers. His was not the life of Thomas Aquinas, sitting in his study with Aristotle's works spread to his left and the Bible and the church teachings spread to his right, quietly recording a massive system for explaining all of God's truth. His was not the life of Martin Luther, leading a spiritual revolution that overturned the economic and political order as well.

Brother Lawrence went to market. He scrubbed vegetables and cleaned fish. He washed dishes. Somehow in the midst of these activities, he became known among his brothers as a peculiarly holy man whose simple counsel on the spiritual life they sought eagerly. Soon secular people who might not otherwise wish to give a moment's nod to a monastery sought him there, drawn to him by his holiness.

A collection of Brother Lawrence's letters, maxims, and some notes on his sayings by an attentive friend comprises *The Practice of the Presence of God*, the brief and simple spiritual classic by which we remember this man. Actually, we do not remember much about him from the book because he says little about his work as a cook or cobbler. He says more about the deep satisfaction of adoring God. He tells about a bare tree in winter and how he became swept up in joy at the promise that the tree would soon bud and grow leaves. Such moments speak volumes about God.

Brother Lawrence entered the order with the single-minded purpose of devoting every moment, every task to loving God. Nothing was too trifling to perform for the love of God, not even picking up a straw from the ground. So he washed dishes for the love of God. He went to market and dickered for peppers and chickens and apples and salt for the love of God. He mopped the floor for the love of God.[1]

In his practical, down-to-earth life, Brother Lawrence saw the truth in Jesus' teachings that most of us miss. When Jesus commanded us to "Love the Lord your God with all your heart, and with all your soul, and with all your strength, and with all your mind; and your neighbor as yourself" (Luke 10:27), he had more than Sunday worship in mind. He had the weekdays and their labors in mind as well.

So my new young friend Tim, kneeling down with an electric saw to cut a hole in my closet floor, seemed a spiritual descendent of Brother Lawrence. The next day I saw him again at lunch time, and I checked to be sure. I asked what he meant when he said that God gives him more work to do while installing air conditioners than God assigns at the church.

He explained that he never dreamed of installing air conditioners as a calling. Rather, he dreamed of traveling and performing Christian concerts for youth. But God had air conditioners in mind, and somehow while he did that work, God kept sending people into his path who wanted to hear what he had to say or to just get a little kindness.

Tim said, "Every other day, I ask God, 'Why do you want me to do this? Why not send me out to do something more fun or exciting?' Every day God gives me a different answer—a person or a need. I don't really know the answer. But I know that Paul had to make tents for a living, and he did a lot of his work for the Lord in the meantime. It keeps me humble, keeps me remembering to follow the Lord."

As for me, Tim keeps me humble. I marvel at the wisdom of this young man. With all of my graduate training and professionalism, I assume that answering God's call at work means planning a career that fulfills my potential and accomplishes great things. Yet, Tim knows that God gives food to the birds and color to the lilies, and on the same token, God gives us meaningful work. We receive it day by day according to God's pleasure, not according to our plan. One must be awake to see it.

Yet, Tim with all his youthful dreams knows that we must plan, that we bear responsibility for choosing our life's work. We need the sense of purpose and mission that work gives us. In *Man's Search for Meaning*, psychiatrist Viktor Frankl's psychological memoir on his captivity in a Nazi concentration camp, he observed that the hope of seeing his wife again gave him a sense of purpose needed for survival. Furthermore, a decision to find meaning and purpose even in the suffering he endured kept him going. Yet, a commitment to his work—his hope of completing a manuscript—also kept him going when all hope of survival seemed lost. When counseling fellow prisoners, he found that reminding them of a purpose for the future—a job to do, a beloved person to see again, or a heightened awareness through suffering—often made the difference between resignation to death or carrying on with life.[2]

We find meaning in work, in relationships, and in the very suffering that can otherwise make life seem futile. In chapter 1, we defined three levels of wakefulness. At the lowest level, we—like the squirrels—work to survive. At the second level, we find meaning in our caring relationships with others. At the highest level, we find our ultimate meaning in abandoning ourselves to God. The quest for meaningful work honors all three levels of wakefulness.

THE SQUIRREL LEVEL: CO-CREATION WITH GOD

Chapter 1 may have left the reader with the impression that God has nothing to do with the squirrels. They just forage for food and flee from potential predators as if no God provides for them or protects them. They live in vigilant anxiety, a far cry from faith.

While I think we must aspire to a wakefulness that exceeds that of squirrels, I do not think that their life of foraging, fleeing, and nesting has nothing to do with God. In order to survive, most of us have no choice but to work, to get our hands dirty in the messy beauty of creation. We may find no more meaning in our work than doing the job and getting paid, grunting through our days with little purpose. Or we may look for God's creative activity in the daily grind. God gives us that choice.

By confronting all living things with the ongoing task of survival, God coaxes all creatures into a collaborative working relationship with the Creator. By making us mortal in a perilous world, God preempted our efforts to go our own way. While working to survive, we always work with God whether or not we acknowledge it. God offers all creatures an honorable part in divine purposes too wonderful for us to know fully.

The Bible begins with God at work, creating the heavens and the earth, separating light from darkness and sea from land, fashioning creeping creatures and flying wonders, giving us air to breathe. With every completed work, God said that it was good. God created Adam and Eve with a job to do—to tend the garden and enjoy it. Likewise, God created the squirrel to nest and play in the trees, to harvest acorns, to be a squirrel. God called both human and squirrel to take part in the ongoing work of creation. That is the first, most basic meaning of work.[3]

When Tim sawed a hole in the floor for a new duct, when Brother Lawrence washed the broccoli and chopped it, they communed with God at the most primordial, unconscious level, the level of creation. God's creative activity constitutes our whole world: Like the sea horse who cannot stand apart from the sea and know what engulfs him, we cannot stand apart from God's creative activity and know its whole meaning. We can only know the job at hand, and like Tim pleading with God to give him more glorious ways to serve, we often carry on without a clue what it means. God said that the creation is good, and we proceed with that assurance.

However, viewing our work as participation in God's good work has limits. First of all, not all work is good. At the sinful extreme, designing cigarette advertisements that target youth, taking pornographic pictures, or legally fighting an urban soup kitchen because it brings "undesirables" uptown hardly constitute good work.

All occupations have moral pitfalls. No career escapes the charge of making an indirect contribution to social harm. When I decided to pursue a career as a counseling psychologist, I thought I chose a field full of milky compassion, devoid of evil. Now thoughtful social critics lay some of the blame for widespread selfishness at psychotherapy's door step.[4] Moreover, my annual malpractice insurance premium grimly reminds me that client-therapist relationships do not always bring sweetness and light.

When creating the world, God declared it good and invited humankind to a vocation of good work. But since the Fall, the goodness of our work bears the same taint as the goodness of our selves. Now we must attentively sift out the good from the bad, the wheat from the chaff in evaluating our labors.

So not all work is good in the moral sense. Moreover, not all work is good in the sense of providing fulfillment and satisfaction for an honest day's labor. I suspect that most of us would quit our jobs if we won the lottery. When Adam sinned, God changed the meaning of work from a privilege to a sentence to work the ground:

> . . . in toil you shall eat of it all the days of your life;
> thorns and thistles it shall bring forth for you;
>> and you shall eat the plants of the field.
> By the sweat of your face
>> you shall eat bread
> until you return to the ground.
>
> (Genesis 3:17-19)

With a lottery check, most of us would try to buy back Eden. Even the good jobs bring their fair share of tedium, distraction, and drudgery. Those who enjoy more than half of their work tasks form an elite group. Most of us find satisfaction in fewer work hours than that. Many bear Adam's curse on assembly lines squirting sugar cream into the middle of cookies or installing springs in car doors.

Only the privileged enjoy the luxury of anxious rumination about finding more meaningful careers. The marketplace challenges us to keep our resumés up-to-date, to keep ourselves either vertically mobile (up the corporate ladder) or horizontally mobile (to another job in another place). Sometimes God issues the same challenges, but often we use the imperative of marketplace mobility to avoid God's call.

God calls us to find meaning in the task at hand, even in the drudgery. Our mobile work culture bids us deal with drudgery, conflict, and inconvenience through escape. Yet in the drudgery, God's face beckons us to come near and challenges us to make room for a coming kingdom through our work, not despite it.

A stack of mail towers before me on my desk. The depression I feel in its shadow has some justification. It is Adam's briar patch. It reminds me that I am not God. My impatience with it confronts me with my vain assumption that I, the all-important one, deserve to use my time in more exalted ways. I must humble myself and read the mail.

Of course, I discard letters into the recycling bin like a riverboat gambler dealing cards. There *are* more important things to do, and I must not use this mundane task to procrastinate. Nevertheless, I cannot wish away this stack of mail, and I must believe that God has a message for me in it—if not a literal message, then an opportunity through the discipline of humble work to see God's handwriting in the details of the day.

We can approach sorting through mail, installing air ducts, or washing dishes as meaningless drudgery or as holy rituals enabling us to abide in the kingdom and see the face of God. God gives us that choice this side of Eden. If we offer our labors to God, God will bless their fruits. Moreover, God will give our labors a place in the creation of the world and in the preparation of a kingdom. No work is too menial or trivial for God to bless in that way. Our drudgery does not limit God's creativity.

God blesses the squirrels and all creatures who work to survive. Yet, God obviously challenges us to get beyond survival mode even in our most tedious tasks. If we strive toward a higher wakefulness, we face the demanding spiritual task of abandoning ourselves to faith in God's creative process amid the drudgery. Few of us can easily make the transition to Brother Lawrence's wakefulness in which he devoted his heart entirely to loving God while he baked a souffle or drained grease from old pans. Therefore, God provides us with helpers in the transition. God provides us with each other.

THE CITIZEN LEVEL:
THE SPIRITUALITY OF WORK RELATIONSHIPS

As discussed above, most of us toil on this side of Eden in work that we enjoy less than half the time.

Much of our work still consists of drudgery and repetition. Yet, some assembly line workers, cooks, and air-conditioning technicians find great satisfaction in their work. Some find satisfaction because they derive a creative challenge where others resign themselves to routine. Yet, most who do work that involves high levels of drudgery gain their satisfaction from relationships with customers and co-workers.

Gregory F. Augustine Pierce edited a collection of essays by lay Christians entitled *Of Human Hands*. In these chapters, the contributors discuss the spirituality of their work. They represent a wide array of careers—an artist, a school system administrator, a data processor, a judge, a newspaper editor, and many more. All offer moving accounts of God's presence in their work. An administrator tells how he experienced God's active presence as he prayed over difficult decisions.[5] An engineer relates that he found God in the surprises that interrupted his world of high efficiency and control.[6] A newspaper editor found divine judgment and mercy in the tension between impersonal professional standards and the loving demands of the gospel.[7]

Virtually all contributors pointed to relationships on the job as the most consistent source of spirituality in their careers. Two contributors struck me especially with their ethic of love on the job because their jobs—supermarket cashier and postal carrier—are not "helping professions" like nursing, social work, counseling, or the pastoral ministry. Maxine F. Dennis, the cashier, wrote an essay entitled, "Compassion Is the Most Vital Tool of My Trade." She described how she uses "observation and perception" to sense the customers' mood and needs of the moment, and she responds accordingly with a kind expression or remark, even with the way she bags the groceries.[8]

Rose Mary Hart, the letter carrier, feels grateful for her job stability because it enables her to establish a relationship of trust with the people whom she serves and with whom she works. She sees how the regularity of her brief visits makes a difference to the people in the community, especially the shut-ins. Conversation about faith flows naturally with everyone in her work life. Speaking out for justice, appropriate evangelizing, and pastoral care fill her work days with a rich abundance that most pastors would envy.[9]

Maxine Dennis and Rose Mary Hart re-enact Jesus' acts in the upper room which reveal the kingdom of God in our midst. As discussed in chapter 2, when Jesus washed his disciples' feet, he showed them the humble servant leadership that characterizes the kingdom. Similarly, when Maxine Dennis bags groceries with compassionate attention to the mood and needs of the customer, she reveals the kingdom. Jesus shared a meal with his disciples. Likewise, when Rose Mary Hart delivers mail to a shut-in, going out of her way to share the hospitality of a personal greeting, she reveals the kingdom.

At work, we can find the kingdom in such small, inconspicuous places. If we open our eyes and awaken, we can see the Maxine Dennises and Rose Mary Harts in our midst, offering their unique holy communion in their labor. If we follow their example and see our work tasks, however small, as opportunities to serve and reveal God's reign, the doing will help us see the kingdom all the more clearly.

Work calls us out of our self-enclosed dreams of fulfillment and forces us into relationships that we might otherwise miss. Yet, work relationships are not always sweet blessings: They can bring more stress than deadlines or heavy-handed personnel policies. Nevertheless, even the most stressful work relationships challenge us to look beyond the job description and the bottom line to see the face of God, the suffering Christ in others.

Work offers an arena for compassion and service, and if the competition or our own fears of intimacy preclude the human dimension, then one must change one's heart or job. The greatest corruption of God's gift of work is not sloth but addiction to work—attention to achievement, money, and the job description so slavish that every human relationship becomes nothing more than a means to an end. Such addiction not only alienates us from our families, co-workers, and friends; it blinds us to the kingdom of God which Jesus placed at the heart of his teaching.

Burnout can occur with a critical dimension of workaholism: the loss of spiritual freedom. After disappointing outcomes or feeling unappreciated, we may see our work as a set of duties rather than opportunities to love and serve God freely and creatively. Too much competitive drive to satisfy an insatiable ego may produce the same result. The best remedy consists of equal doses of psychological self-care and prayer—especially prayer that offers up the enslaving ego in a ritual of sacrifice to the liberating God.

Earlier, we saw that we cannot sustain the spirituality of co-creation with God at the squirrel level of wakefulness without striving for a higher wakefulness. Similarly, the spirituality of compassionate service at the citizen level of wakefulness cannot maintain itself without striving for the highest wakefulness. Burn-out or workaholism will follow for most of us who do not abandon ourselves prayerfully to God in our work. Thus, we return to Brother Lawrence.

THE HIGHEST WAKEFULNESS: LOVING GOD AT WORK

Brother Lawrence said "That it was a great delusion to think that time set aside for prayer should be different from other times, that we were equally obliged to be united to God by work in the time assigned to work as by prayer during prayertime."[10] For Brother Lawrence, turning to God in prayer or at work took the same kind of effort:

> During our work and other activities, during our spiritual reading and writing, yes, even more so during our formal devotions and spoken prayers, we should stop as often as we can, for a moment, to adore God from the bottom of our hearts, to savor Him as it were, as He passes by. Since you know God is with you in all your actions, that He is in the deepest recesses of your soul, why not, from time to time, leave off your external activities, and even your spoken prayers to adore Him inwardly, to praise Him, to petition Him, to offer Him your heart and to thank Him?[11]

Brother Lawrence found meaning in the drudgery

and in the community by keeping alive his conversation with God. There was meaning in the drudgery because God was there. There was meaning in the community because God was there. Neither the labors nor the people enslaved him. He went about his business in subtle detachment, attending primarily to God. Yet, in doing so, he saw the meaning in the work all the clearer.

If I go to the shore, walk a few feet into the waves, and look straight down, I will see water. If I look up to the rim of the horizon, I will see the ocean. I see the ocean much more clearly by looking beyond it than by looking straight at it.

So it is with our work. If I look straight at the task, I will see drudgery. If I look beyond the task to God, I will see God's creative work. If I look straight at a customer or co-worker, I see a person making demands. If I look beyond the customer or co-worker to God, I will see Christ in the eyes of the person before me.

One caught up in the highest wakefulness finds meaning in work by looking beyond work to God for meaning. Our work obtains meaning when we participate in God's creative work. God gives our work meaning by blessing our work relationships with Christ's presence. Yet, a pursuit of meaning exclusively through work will disappoint us. We must allow ourselves moments of inner adoration, turning our hearts solely to God.

There is method in this madness. Luke 10:38-42 (NIV) tells the story of Mary and Martha:

> As Jesus and his disciples were on their way, he came to a village where a woman

named Martha opened her home to him. She had a sister called Mary, who sat at the Lord's feet listening to what he said. But Martha was distracted by all the preparations that had to be made. She came to him and asked, "Lord, don't you care that my sister has left me to do the work by myself? Tell her to help me!" "Martha, Martha," the Lord answered, "you are worried and upset about many things, but only one thing is needed. Mary has chosen what is better, and it will not be taken away from her."

The madness lies in trying to integrate the Martha and the Mary in oneself. This task may seem impossible because much work and responsibility distract most of us like Martha. The busyness enables us to escape from our highest calling: adoring God. Mary fulfilled that calling during Jesus' visit, and all of us, like Mary, long to see God's face.

At first blush, the story seems to set up work and worship as mutually exclusive, either/or options. Yet, Brother Lawrence showed us that the two can blend, that one can do Martha's work in the kitchen and adore God at once. For Brother Lawrence, work was a form of worship. He offered both to God in praise. If integrating Mary and Martha within ourselves is the madness, the method consists of offering our work to God in worship just as we offer our prayers.

Doing our work as an act of worship helps us to see God. This can mean offering the fruits of our labor as a gift to God. In the first act of worship recorded in the Bible, a cattleman offered meat and a farmer offered produce to God (Genesis 4:3-4). The best outcome of our work—cool air in homes, effective educational programs, financial stability for clients, cheerful customers, or countless other possibilities—can help us to see the God to whom we offer them.

Moreover, it helps not only to offer the fruits or outcomes of our labor, but the labor itself. One can dance to praise God, but one cannot freeze or bottle the dance and keep it on a shelf. The dance glorifies God in the act itself. We can offer our work as the dancer offers the dance, an act of worship that seeks no utilitarian justification, only the glory of God. Through our work, we can heed Rabbi Heschel's challenge to live our lives as if they were works of art, and like good works of art, our lives will help us and those around us to see. If we devote our work to God, we will see God's face, and others may see intimations of God in our labor.

Full-time Work and Devotion: Concluding Perspectives

Beginning the day with spiritual exercises such as Bible study, meditation, and prayer supports higher wakefulness at work. The shrimp fisherman who admires the stars and the moonlight dancing on the waves before hauling in the evening's catch will appreciate the wonder of the labor more than the one who spends the dark hours anxiously worrying about the volume in the nets. One who adores God and offers petitions to the Lord before facing the day's demands will find greater meaning in work and love than one who is too busy to pause.

This chapter's suggestions for living wakefully at work may sound like too much piety to sustain on the job. The life of full-time devotion reveals how the clutter and pressure of work preoccupy us. The more we turn our hearts to God during the push and pull of our work days, the more painfully we realize how much we withdraw from God. "You are worried and distracted by many things," we hear Jesus chide.

This will discourage us about higher wakefulness only if we seek our own perfection and not God for God's sake. Brother Lawrence placed a premium on devoting one's life to God for God's sake, not for the sake of one's own gain on earth or in heaven. Thus, Brother Lawrence could take moments with God in the kitchen and savor those moments without undue guilt for the stretches of time he might have not thought of God. All that matters is God in that moment.

If the drudgery of work teaches humility as carving holes for ducts did for my friend Tim, higher wakefulness teaches humility all the more. It reveals that only God's faithfulness is constant; ours is at best fleeting. "Blessed are the poor in spirit, for theirs is the kingdom of heaven" (Matthew 5:3). The poor in spirit know the poverty of their faith, the transience of their wakefulness. Yet, theirs is the kingdom of heaven. With patience and persistence, we will reap the fruits of God's training in faithfulness. We will not only see the kingdom amid the drudgery; we will abide in it.

A psalm offers the last word on meaningful work:

Unless the LORD builds the house,
    those who build it labor in vain.

Unless the LORD guards the city,
    the guard keeps watch in vain.
It is in vain that you rise up early
    and go late to rest,
eating the bread of anxious toil;
    for he provides for his beloved during sleep.
                         (Psalm 127:1-2)[12]

Work is not the primary source of meaning in life. It is not even the source of our security. God is the source of meaning and security. God creates us and all of our hours. God appoints our tasks and our rest. God blesses us whole, not just our work achievements, our paychecks, our pats on the back. Thus, we turn in the remaining chapters to life at home and together, at play and rest to explore what it means to live a wakeful faith.

QUESTIONS FOR REFLECTION AND DISCUSSION

1. What gives you the greatest sense of creative accomplishment in your work? What do you find most tedious? How do you find God working in both the achievements and drudgery of your job?

2. Review the section in chapter 2 entitled, "What the Kingdom Looks Like." Reflect on your relationships with co-workers, customers, and clients in light of Jesus' actions in the upper room with his disciples. How does your behavior with others at work resemble Jesus' behavior in the upper room? How could you make your relationships at work look more like the kingdom of God?

3. Reflect on a time at work when your heart turned to God by accident. Perhaps a crisis or somebody's words brought it on. How could you repeat that moment of communion with God by choice? How often could you do it?

CHAPTER 10

Keeping House

A LEGACY OF RESTLESSNESS

As that great American film *The Wizard of Oz* draws to a close, Dorothy concludes her journey down the Yellow Brick Road not by crossing a finish line or riding an air balloon into the heavens, but by closing her eyes and repeating, "There's no place like home. There's no place like home." It works. She opens her eyes soon enough to find herself in bed with a cold cloth on her forehead, Auntie Em, the farm hands, and her dog Toto attending to her. Whether it was an elaborate dream or a journey into another dimension, she traveled far, endured much peril, and finally arrived at the place of her deepest longing.

Ironically, once she cleared the cobwebs and realized that her wish to return home came true, she immediately told the story of a faraway place called Oz. She told the farm hands that they were there as a cowardly lion, a tin man, and a scarecrow, her companions seeking their destinies as well. They endured the guerrilla tactics of a wicked witch and her corps of flying monkeys and guardian trees. Once Dorothy landed at home, she could talk about little more than this place away from home with its villains and fellow dreamers.

It is an American story line if ever there was one. Whether they came voluntarily or involuntarily, our ancestors who journeyed here all faced unspeakable peril, and all longed for home, a place to tell about their adventures, a place to belong at last. Our ancestors left home in hopes of finding home, set out on a journey with the dream of ultimately claiming a place to find their mind, their heart, their courage, their true home.

We love the adventure; yet, we love home. We want a place to end the search and tell about it, but we inherited restless souls. We move from house to house, community to community, still seeking our fortunes, our final destinies. It makes for a lonely land teeming with rootless people.

Perhaps that explains how biblical faith endures for some Americans despite the secularizing pressures of marketplace and technology. We inherited the soul of Abraham, that old man who traded in his acceptance letter to the retirement home for a passport to God-knows-where. We share his longing for a place of promise, and the adventure to that place defines our faith.

Of course, many of us settle in the suburbs, chaining ourselves to ungodly house payments. Yet, we justify those payments as investments, and we maintain the house to enhance its resale value. Even if we stay for decades, we spend most of that time with one eye on the road. Like Dorothy or Abraham, we long for home, but we know that our legacy lies in the journey, the search.

This makes home a spiritually challenging place. Couple American restlessness with biblical stories of Abraham's quest, the return of Israel under Moses' leadership, and the travels of Jesus and Paul, and it should surprise no one that we think of the spiritual life as a journey. Of course, the spiritual life *is* a journey, but unless we develop practical ways to venture out spiritually while we keep house, television will monopolize our attention at dinner time. The insatiable quest for material luxury will dominate our domestic plans. The God who calls us on our journeys and prepares for us a home will have no place there.

"Our hearts are restless until they rest in thee," Augustine prayed. Restlessness is not peculiarly American, but universal. The need to accept our God-given homes as places where we can ease our restless hearts and rest in God's care undergirds the spirituality of life at home.

We also wait for God at home. We wait for the kingdom's coming. We look out the window and watch. The Christian settles in an earthly home as a provisional place, an outpost for pilgrims. The need to make our homes places of preparation for changes and new ventures draws the spirituality of life at home into the spirituality of the journey.

The house we keep is not our ultimate destiny, but it is the place God made for us today. In it we can enact the rituals of arrival, of waking up in our own bed and seeing Christ attending to us and listening to our story. Life at home becomes a parable of the kingdom, and keeping house offers many rich but inconspicuous opportunities to live our lives as works of art that glorify God.

Making Shalom

The Hebrew salutation *Shalom* blesses our neighbor with a wish for more than a good day. *Shalom* means "have a whole, complete, rich life." It wishes peace, but more than mere absence of conflict. The peace of *shalom* makes room for growth, relationships, and pursuit of our dreams. By wishing a friend *shalom*, we say not only, "Take care of yourself," but also, "May God take care of you."

God wishes *shalom* for each of us. God gave Adam and Eve *shalom* in the form of the Garden of Eden. When God dismissed them from the garden, the divine wish for *shalom* did not end. But since Eden, *shalom* requires waiting for God while cultivating home as a provisional Eden.

That is tricky business. It entails two seemingly contradictory imperatives: Honor God's will for your well-being by taking care of yourself, and make yourself at home in God's creation. Meanwhile, deny yourself, take up your cross, and follow Jesus to the kingdom.

Take care of yourself. Deny yourself. Christian history consists of movements emphasizing one or the other of these imperatives, and each movement founders on their excesses. Through the rituals of keeping house, God helps us to find the balance, to enjoy the fruits of the garden while waiting through the pain of life for the kingdom's coming.

I write these words after a weekend of heavy housekeeping. Through a couple of loads of dishes and several loads of clothes, my wife and I sorted and scrubbed and soaped away germs and grime. We will re-enter the clean dishes and fresh clothes into the filthy cycle of life, washing them again before long.

We bought groceries and cooked and ate and stored leftovers. Everything we ate from the potatoes to the meat loaf had to die to give us life. The groceries come in a never-ending train in this abundant land, and we do our share of the work. They give us life as our bodies age in imperceptible increments, slowly dying.

I spent the better part of a day in the hot, dusty attic, clearing out clutter, biting my lip as I boxed up beloved books to take to the library or college notebooks to take to the dumpster. Out went old clothes, broken appliances, items we bought with high hopes only to forget them. I found it hard at first to let them go. Maybe we will need them. Maybe we will want to revisit them. These are not my children, I chided myself. They are only relics of the past, and the past is gone.

With my wife's help, I envisioned a more functional organization of the attic, and I moved the remaining furniture and boxes into their new places. There is more room up there now, room for the future with its books and clothes and forgotten things. We will try to keep the clutter in check, but we cannot stave off the future's tide with all its stuff, the things cannot yet throw away because we cannot grieve the passing of the days fast enough.

I did it for my wife. I did it for the child we expect, the precious one we need to make room for, but I did it also for myself. I dreaded this housework, but I cannot deny the satisfaction of seeing more space to move and breathe in. I like the new life in old wood where I swept away the dust accumulated from years of my inattentiveness.

I would rather write or make love or explore new country. Nevertheless, cleaning, eating, mowing grass, and uncluttering immerse me in the cycles of time, of growing and decaying, living and dying. The dishes and potatoes and books and floorboards and I all do it together, gather the residue of time, discard it and move on. Eventually, we become time's residue and death dismisses us as history goes on.

Take care of yourself. Deny yourself. The two commands seem all of a piece in the attic as I sort through books or in the kitchen as I scour the sauce pans. This is where I take care of myself. This is where I deny myself. This is where I wait for God as time marches on.

HOSPITALITY AND STEWARDSHIP

Self-care is spiritually dangerous. It easily degenerates into selfishness. The self-help section in the local bookstore offers a shrine to the self. Books by charismatic Ph.D.'s tell us how to climb the corporate or social ladder with greater ease, take anyone we wish to bed, or believe in ourselves. Much of what we find there can support spiritually disciplined self-care, but much of it also caters to the narcissism that gets in the way of wakefulness.

This book's leading metaphor suggests that spiritual growth ascends in three stages of wakefulness. At the lowest stage, we, like the squirrels, hustle to survive and ward off threat. Much of what passes for prosperity in our culture does not rise above this stage. Conspicuous consumption and status-seeking drive more of our actions than most of us care to admit, with self-preservation as the root motive. Yet, acts of self-preservation, as when we clean house, can have spiritual content if we let our concern not only include the self but extend beyond it.

Moving beyond the self propels us to the next stage. At the citizen level of wakefulness, we find meaning in caring relations with others. No socially isolated self exists. The best modern personality theorists embed the self in a context of relationships. What we think others think of us—or what we think they would think of us if they really knew us—shapes our self-concept. Our relationship with ourselves parallels the ways we believe others relate to us. Thus, self-care requires making room in our lives for others.

As we keep house, we must literally make room for others, even if we live alone. The furniture arrangement in the sitting room must allow for conversation, not just television viewing. The dinner table requires an inviting setting to share a meal together. "Do not neglect to show hospitality to strangers, for thereby some have entertained angels unawares" (Hebrews 13:2, RSV). Even those who live alone without expecting guests may keep a hospitable home environment as a ritual exercise in wakeful expectation of unannounced holiness.

Keeping house at the citizen level of wakefulness means keeping an open house, one that invites the world in and that offers a secure base for venturing out. This helps us to take care of ourselves and keep our eyes open to Christ in the neighbor or stranger. It helps us also to nurture the joyful spirituality of stewardship.

Stewardship means taking care of property entrusted to oneself. In the eyes of the state and the banks, many of us own our homes. Yet, God sees us all as renters—or perhaps more precisely, guests or house sitters. Our homes are not our own. God entrusted them to us, and as we keep house we must pause periodically to reflect on God's calling not only for our selves, but for our homes and those who visit there.

When Jesus washed his disciples' feet and broke bread with them, he gave them a picture of the kingdom as a place of hospitality. Keeping house with the visitor in mind can be a parable of the kingdom. Through it the visitor may catch a glimpse of the kingdom. God entrusts our homes to us in order to proclaim the kingdom, and the mundane routines of cleaning and rearranging and decorating can serve that purpose.

Of course, perfectionistic housekeeping may not say as much about the kingdom as it says about the housekeeper. The host who watches every dust particle with anxiety or who can hardly contain dismay over muddy shoes misses the point. *Better Homes and Gardens* magazine does not display the kingdom. Rather, one must create an environment physically conducive to intimacy, one that expresses the host's faith. For some, that may entail a Spartan, rustic home. For others, it may entail carefully selected art. Still others may intentionally keep the house looking "lived in." Keeping house is part of living life as a work of art, but one must not make the house so perfect or imposing that it precludes relaxed, mutual conversation.

At the citizen level, keeping house serves as an extension of caring for others. One cleans up after dinner with the same spirit with which one welcomes a visitor in church. Both contribute to the mission of hospitality. Yet, that mission can degenerate into etiquette for the sake of status unless one moves farther still from the self and wakefully watches for the mark of God's hand in the woodwork, the lighting, the details of home as memories accumulate there.

DOMESTIC HOLINESS

We can keep house and make home a hospitable place. But can we make it holy? Of holiness, Frederick Buechner writes: "Only God is holy, just as only people are human. God's holiness is his Godness. To speak of anything else as holy is to say that it has something of God's mark upon it. Times, places, things, and people can all be holy, and when they are, they are usually not hard to recognize."[1]

Can we make our homes holy? Taking Buechner's perspective, we cannot. Only God can make our homes holy. The most wakeful among us rest assured that no home escapes God's creative hand, making all the world including our homes holy. All homes contain the stuff of holiness. The question is whether we are awake enough to see it.

Buechner describes a place he considers holy, a dimly lit workshop complete with a makeshift wood-burning stove, a workbench that doubles as a cat's quarters, tools, work clothes, a mud-caked bulldozer, and lots of broken things. The place smells of smoke and oil. It sounds like grandpa's shed out back, full of memories and evidence of a life lived close to the soil.[2]

Buechner wisely claims that he has no idea why the place is holy.[3] He may have ideas, but explanations of holiness always fall short. Perhaps every tool and broken thing and piece of equipment carry cherished memories. Perhaps he knows a saint who faithfully worked there, forging a home and a soul with hard labor. Perhaps he hears God in the silence of the place. Yet, none of these possibilities suffice to explain the workshop's holiness. Nothing fully explains the mark of God and how we recognize it.

"I have no idea why this place is holy, but you can tell it is the moment you set foot in it *if you have an eye for that kind of thing*," Buechner writes (emphasis mine).[4] If you have an eye for that kind of thing: That phrase gets to the crux of the matter for our purposes. We will not necessarily make our homes any more holy by putting a crucifix or a picture of baby Jesus or a needlepoint prayer on the wall. Stocking our book shelves with theological volumes will not do. We must develop an eye for holiness so we can see how God already makes our tool sheds and linen closets and guest rooms holy.

Abraham Joshua Heschel advised that we live our lives as if they were works of art. God creates the meaningful shape of our lives, and leaving us the task of seeing and then revealing that shape. We set it free like a sculptor chipping away the rock that encases a beautiful figure.

Seeing our homes from the perspective of higher wakefulness is like a sculptor eyeing a slab of granite. A shape inheres there, a meaningful figure. It is the mark of God. One can see it the way Buechner saw holiness in the old workshop. Like a sculptor, one must cultivate the eye for it.

Our idiom for abiding in a home states that we "live there." The phrase goes in one ear and out the other because we say it and hear it so much. Yet, it says a great deal. It says that we eat there, laugh there, talk on the phone, balance the check book, make love, grieve, sleep, and brush our teeth there. What we do helps us to see, and doing what we do in obedience to God's calling helps us to see God's face, or in Buechner's term for holiness, obedience helps us see the mark of God.

Brother Lawrence saw the mark of God in the pots and pans hanging from pegs on a wooden rack. He saw holiness in the veneer of grease that built up on the stone wall about the oven; in the old cat with half a tail who visited when Lawrence cooked fish; in the green and red and yellow of the vegetables. He heard holiness in the crackling of fire, the sizzling of fish, the laughter and cross words and murmurs and sighs of brothers outside the kitchen door as meal time arrived. He smelled holiness in the soap and water, in the wet stone work after he scrubbed off the grimy veneer, in the fresh cut broccoli and the bucket of grease.

He saw, heard, and smelled the holiness that he tasted as well when he joined his brothers for a meal. He touched it in the cold, hard, common table and the shoulder clasp of a grateful friend. Brother Lawrence took in the holiness of the place because he lived the holiness.

In this age of psychology, we might cheapen this by saying holiness is all a matter of attitude, but it is not. It is *really* there, in the monastery kitchen many years ago and in our homes today. Those who deny themselves understand: The holiness in which they immerse themselves through obedience precedes them and they submit to it. Those who take care of themselves understand: In attending to the details of the place that God appointed them to keep, they find God in the concrete particularities and peculiarities of home.

So home is a place of adventure for the most wakeful. It is the setting for a journey full of discovery and surprise. It is not always safe, and it is not always desirable for it to be safe. At home we walk the Yellow Brick Road, search for the promised land, and find it if we have an eye for that kind of thing. When God calls, not even our four walls shelter us from the journey. God reveals enough wonders even in the routines of keeping house until God calls us out the door and we find God's face in the world.

QUESTIONS FOR REFLECTION AND DISCUSSION

1. Which household task do you most enjoy? In doing it, how do you deny yourself? How do you take care of yourself? Now consider the household task that you least enjoy, and answer the same questions. Compare the ways God addresses you in each task.

2. When you expect visitors in your home, what do you do to prepare your house for them? How do you feel as you prepare? How does your experience of preparation affect the visit?

3. Describe a holy place at your home. Go to that place and pray, naming every detail in your description and thanking God for it. If you read this chapter as a member of a study group, let all group members share these descriptions. When you share your description, do not try to explain why the place is holy. Let your listeners tell you how they hear holiness in your description.

CHAPTER 11

Family Vocations

In *Finding God at Home: Family Life as Spiritual Discipline*, Ernest Boyer, Jr. opens with a striking image that appears to lack any relevance to the family. He describes Skellig Michael, a granite island six miles off the coast of Ireland. This massive rock with its towering peaks and craggy cliffs juts defiantly out of the dark sea, daring the tide to thrash it, daring humans to cross the water and walk it. Skellig Michael is an outpost from land and the comforts of civilized life.

Yet, around the sixth century, Christian hermits inhabited it for over one hundred years. These hermits forsook everything and lived on that tiny island in prayer and meditation. They sought the face of God amid rock and sky and sea. They sought the kingdom in the cold and exposure and loneliness of Skellig Michael.[1]

Such a life seems madness to most, but God calls a few to the rigors of such lonely places. More often, God calls peculiar saints to the desert, which is all the same as Skellig Michael in the end. God calls them to places where nothing but demons can distract them from the Face for which they pine.

The demons come out in force, so I hear. The records of monastic lives bear out the terrors that visit in deep solitude. The body's desire for sensual pleasure, the mind's craving for stimulation and fancy, the ego's ravenous hunger for recognition turn upon the hermit in fierce backlashes of torment. Jesus faced these torments for forty days and forty nights. Saint Antony faced them for twenty years. Yet, for the holy hermit who remains steadfast in prayer, who keeps awake for God's reign in no-man's-land, the demons only burn away the refuse that blocks the view of God. The face of God appears to those who wait.

Boyer calls this "the spirituality of the edge," a spirituality for those who seek God at the edge of society and sanity. Children have no place on the edge. The few called and the fewer who endure focus their energies on one bond and one bond only: the bond with God. In doing so, God leads them to a deeper love for humanity, but always from afar, always from the edge.

The great spiritual insights of Christianity and other faiths originate so often from such solitary lives of harsh devotion that "a spirituality of the family" may seem awkwardly out of place. The New Testament does not make it much easier: Jesus challenged his disciples several times to place devotion to him above devotion to family (e.g., Matthew 10:37, 12:48-50; Luke 9:59-60). Paul spoke in superior tones of his single life, deeming marriage an encumbering compromise between the Christian calling and the demands of the flesh (1 Corinthians 7:7-9).

Yet, Skellig Michael gives Boyer his leading image for the spirituality of the family because he found in his family life striking parallels to spiritual life on the edge. In the hermit seeking shelter from the bitter wind and the father listening to his four-year-old tell the same knock-knock joke for the forty-second time, Boyer found the same elements of spiritual growth: a call, preparation to respond, wrestling with demons, and finally the vision of the face of God.[2]

Although much more common than the life of secluded prayer, family life is no less a calling. A calling is not a job description. It is the task God assigns through which one helps prepare the world for the kingdom's coming. "The place God calls you to is the place where your deep gladness and the world's deep hunger meet," Frederick Buechner writes.[3] One works out a calling in the family no less than in a career.

How many marriages go flat because one or both partners see marriage as simply something that normal people do sooner or later, as just a function of average existence like sleeping or dressing in the morning? How many children grow up lonely or angry because their parents brought them into this world to fill the family quota of two or three children? In our family life, God calls us not to collect family members and put them on display like two cars and a house in the suburbs. God calls us to love each as a unique individual. God calls us to walk the road of loving as a venture into uncharted territory, full of perils and wonders.

In practical terms, there is no sufficient reason to marry anyone. Sexual attractiveness offers fleeting satisfactions. A shared work ethic will suffice only for those who see their home as a domestic business. Witty conversation can help the time pass if passing the time is all you want. Yet, whatever our reasons for marrying, God calls us together for mysterious reasons that it will take a lifetime of love to discern.

Cold calculation offers even less reason to have children. Many of us need to nurture little ones, but that need seems rather embarrassing while the child pitches a screaming tantrum in the pasta aisle of the local supermarket. We enjoy seeing our physical traits in the ones we conceived or our mannerisms in the ones we adopted, but if that's the chief joy of having children, we might as well join Narcissus by the pond. Yet, God calls us to raise a particular child with a cowlick and peanut butter chin, and God reveals the reasons as we walk with that child through the simple joys and uncanny vicissitudes of growing up.

Once we respond to the call to marriage and parenthood, we must face the demons. Given the state of the family in our culture, one finds plenty of evidence that demons await us in family life once we heed the call. More than half of all marriages end in divorce. Social scientists trace bold links connecting broken families with poverty, academic under-achievement, and juvenile delinquency. Intact couples feel the pressures of increasing economic demands that lure them ever more into the work place and away from their children and each other. Television—with its dumbed-down culture of obsessive sex, violence, and immediate gratification—serves as our number one baby-sitter.

Simple forgetfulness of our calling probably accounts for much of this strain and decay, but any devoted spouse or parent knows that the demons come with many more faces. Resentments build up with the loss of peace and quiet, with the compromises, with the money spent that we would have just as soon saved or the money saved that we would have just as soon spent. Moreover, we cultivate family ties at the expense of many dreams. We do not take the career risks we might have otherwise taken, write the novel we hoped to write, embrace the lover we dreamed of embracing, sought the pot of gold at the end of the rainbow. There are bills to pay, mouths to feed, time to share before time runs out.

The demons of lost dreams grow to monstrous proportions in this age of delusion. "MasterCard, I'm bored," a celebrity complains on an old commercial, and with his MasterCard to help him, he travels to exotic places, stays in the finest hotels, consorts with the loveliest ladies. Television and other media saturate us with this delusion that we can have it all—and that we should want it all and that something is wrong with us if we do not. It is an easy delusion to sell in the richest, most powerful nation in history, a nation in which the common person enjoys luxuries that would drive an ancient Egyptian pharaoh mad with envy.

We buy the delusion that we can and should have it all more than we know. We unconsciously buy this delusion about ten times as much as we consciously think we do. Our culture's pressured pursuit of shallow, ephemeral fantasies makes it hard to cultivate a deep and lasting love that "bears all things, believes all things, hopes all things, endures all things" (1 Corinthians 13:7).

Other dreams can suck the blood out of our family ties. What married person did not have to unlearn ideals of the bride or groom that no one can live up to? What parent did not have to relearn the hard way how a child thinks (or does not think) when order and harmony seem painfully out of reach? It takes a love greater than anything we can manufacture to endure these losses and disappointments.

Moreover, it takes a joy greater than any we ever imagined to make us—gray, wrinkled, and older—look past the post-honeymoon cold wars and the ugly adolescent rebellions and say, "It was all worth it. I would do it all again." Nothing is more astonishing and moving than the frequency with which we say that in our twilight years. We get into family commitments in utter foolishness, blind to the demons. We get out of them wisdom and joy that open our eyes to the divine.

The face of God appears for moments in the familiar faces of our family members, or at least God appears not far over their shoulders, watching us, watching over the love that we share. We watch a son play countless baseball games on hot summer days. We endure long arthritic weeks with an aging parent. We journey through long years and decades with a husband whose hair loss marks their passing. If we do it for the duration, a mystery appears in our memories of family times. God, we find, walked with us all along, and we can remember God in those faces we love for no good reason except that God put them in our lives, made them who they are, and called us to love them.

We love despite the demons that invade our families, and we see or anticipate the face of God at the end of the journey. So we will take guidance from Boyer's point: The spiritual quest of family life follows a parallel course with the spiritual quest of the ancient hermit on Skellig Michael. We respond to God's call. We struggle with demons. We see God's face in our final destiny.

MARRIAGE

Marital love parallels the three stages of spiritual wakefulness described in the first chapter. It begins with sexual craving, evolves to deeper appreciation of the partner's humanity, and culminates as the love we share reveals God. The more we submit ourselves to the growing love between us, the closer we draw to the consuming Source of love beyond us.

The love we share in marriage exceeds the sum of the neurochemicals stimulated in sexual attraction. It means more than the exchange of sexual and economic resources between two people differently endowed by nature and custom. True marital love intrudes upon us from without. It brings joy more staggering than we imagined and sorrow deeper than we ever feared.

Given our culture's boredom with marriage, such lofty words may seem rather antique. Our love stories end with the wedding, not with the second mortgage. Marriages drift apart, and we run out of energy to know our partner more deeply. We conclude that we know enough about the one who once mystified us, so we turn to other things.

Such drift and boredom results directly from our refusal to invite God into our marriages. It exposes our subtle atheism: We do not believe in intimate wonders beyond those our hormones supply. We do not believe that the face of this one with whom we argued over the grocery bill, the layout of the new living room, or the affair of the heart (if not the body) can reveal the face of God.

In a sense, such atheism has a point. Our spouse's face may not reveal God's face, especially after all that. Yet, God will reveal our beloved's face if we invite God in, and in seeing our beloved anew after many years of marriage, we can see the face of God moving to the foreground.

Life is full of suffering, and married life is full of suffering together. Love heightens the suffering, but also the hope. Jesus promised the kingdom to those who suffer in his name (Matthew 5:10-12). Those who love each other in Jesus' name, who pray together and worship together and laugh and keep house and make love and grieve together in his name, will find at the end of life's suffering that their love is a jewel they could not have fashioned if they tried. They will find that their love did not begin with hormones after all but with grace, God's self-giving reach. They will know that God is love.

PARENTHOOD

Paul Wilkes knew his life fell short. His work and pastimes seemed to lead to nothing special. He drifted in a sea of mediocrity. So he broke up with the woman he was dating, cast aside his career as a writer and film maker, and took up what he hoped was his calling—life as a hermit outside a monastery gate. He wrote, "I wanted to hear a call more than I can remember wanting anything in my life. I was sure my life then would not only have meaning, but would also make enormous sense and, certainly, be most worthwhile."[4]

He lived the rituals of prayer, meditation, and mortification with the brothers by day, and he retreated to his hermitage in the evening for more prayer and labor alone. He liked the discipline that previously seemed to escape him. The monk's life appeared to fit. God should have called him, the fit seemed so right. But the call to the monastic life never came.

Or more precisely, the monastic call did come, but not as he expected. God called Paul Wilkes to the monastic labor called parenthood: "Little did I know that the monastic life was only a wedding ring away and that the insights into monastic life I'd had in the year at [the monastery] would be refocused (and only slightly refracted) in married life."[5] He returned to the woman he left before, they married, and he became a father.

In his article, "A Monk in the Bosom of His Family," Wilkes writes of the holy rigors and unexpected graces of raising two sons, Noah and Daniel, ages four and two respectively. His days no longer punctuated by set times for prayer, labor, reading, and journaling, the order of the day now follows the rhythm of naps, meals, and diaper changes. As the monk takes up his cross by diminishing his will, the parent forsakes the selfish will for tending a fever, playing a game of horsy, and spooning baby food.[6]

Parenting is the most sublime expression of that second level of spirituality we have called the citizen level. We find meaning in our lives in glances and gazes exchanged from the moment our child opens those puffy little eyes to search our face to the moment we look through the fog of tears and say that last good-bye before death. We protect and nurture this person with more strength and fortitude than we ever imagined finding in our guts. We relinquish control as we go, almost always underestimating or overestimating the aspiring adult's readiness.

The child must live life as if it were a work of art. Whether the child ends up in medical school or skid row, we cannot ultimately accept credit or blame. We can only make a home, offer our arms and our ears, provide the time and space and discipline and loving presence for the artist to work. In so opening ourselves to the mystery of God's work in our child's life, we move on to the highest wakefulness.

Like the monk, the parent heeds a calling of self-denial, of dedication to the life of another. The children come first, even before the self. Parenthood is a parable of the kingdom of which Jesus taught, "Those who want to save their life will lose it, and those who lose their life for my sake will find it" (Matthew 16:25). This parable does not reveal a codependency trap, a grim existence of compulsive suffering and martyrdom. This parable, despite its trials and tedium, reveals joy that only the monk or the parent can understand. Liberated from the self's grandiose demands, the parent and the monk are free to love, and by loving we find our life.

Forsaking all in the search for God's face, the monk develops a deep love for humanity. Forsaking oneself to love a child, the parent sees the face of God. The monk and the parent walk their lives in a great circle in opposite directions, arriving at the same divine place in the end.

CHILDHOOD

This chapter has focused on the mid-life spiritual callings of the family. Yet, childhood, as we already see, profoundly affects the spiritual lives of others, and Jesus points to children as spiritual guides: "Let the little children come to me; do not stop them; for it is to such as these that the kingdom of God belongs. Truly I tell you, whoever does not receive the kingdom of God as a little child will never enter it" (Mark 10:14-15). The vocation of children is spontaneous trust. Their protection by parents and society enables children to fulfill their calling.

Anyone who follows the news knows how tragically we fall short in enabling children to fulfill their vocation. Poverty and malnutrition scar for life countless children in the United States and abroad. The physical, emotional, and sexual abuses of children seem commonplace. For good reason, conscientious parents warn their children not to talk with strangers, a necessary evil as old as evil itself. Every act that compromises the safety and security of children diminishes all children spiritually. Furthermore, we lose the benefits of the most vital ministry of all, the ministry of childhood.

What is the ministry of childhood? To answer that, we must first look at the chief spiritual pitfall of adulthood: Adults have great difficulty accepting grace. We learned to walk and feed ourselves and talk long ago, and learning to see ourselves as competent and self-sufficient only begins there. We warm up to the image of ourselves as masters of our destinies, and we do not need hand outs. We know we are not perfect, but we consider ourselves good enough. We can certainly point to others worse than us. Such armor around our egos develops as we grow up, an armor that will not let grace in.

Jesus calls us to be as little children, and perhaps that takes a life on the edge for adults. It takes a desert discipline, relinquishing the layers of armor that offer false security apart from grace. Honest openness to grace comes easily only for children. Children teach us by example. The spontaneous love and unashamed dependence of children keep before us a living lesson on receiving God's love. Moreover, their spontaneous love reveals the love of our Father.

Jesus told a story of a child come of age, a young adult who had to relearn childhood. The prodigal son took his inheritance and squandered it in exotic and erotic places. Only when reduced to the life of the lowest farm hand did he strip off the armor. Standing in the mud with hands and pockets full of pig feed, he admitted that he could not manage his own life. So he returned to his father.

The prodigal hit bottom, grieving the loss of his undeserved security until he could do nothing other than accept grace. But the parable is not over, and it is not ultimately about the son. It is about the father. When the father saw his haggard son plodding home at a distance, the father ran to greet him, embraced him, and started arranging a welcome home party for his stunned son before they could unwrap their arms from around each other. The father loved with the spontaneity of a child (Luke 15:11-24).

With such love, God loves us. With such love, God prepares us for the feast to celebrate our return. In adulthood we tend to stray far away, delude ourselves that we can build a life of our own. With that delusion, the serpent enticed Eve to take the forbidden fruit (Genesis 3:4-5). God calls us with the spontaneity of a child and the grace of a loving Father. Somehow we catch a glimpse of the Father running to greet us, and we feel like a child again. We remember what we learned in our former vocation of childhood, and we begin to grow as if born again, loving God with a godlike, childlike love.

Earlier in this chapter, I mentioned Jesus' rather negative slant on the family as he taught his disciples to place devotion to him and the kingdom ahead of family matters. Yet, Jesus' positive slant on the family comes with his use of a familial image when talking about our relationship with God. "Our Father," he began the Lord's Prayer, and "Abba, Father," he prayed in the anguish of Gethsemane. As a child, he addressed God and waited for the love of a Father.

AGING

As their powers and faculties diminish, our elders offer a ministry much like that of children: a ministry of dependence. If the child offers a parable of the spontaneous, joyful dependence that accepts grace, the older person offers a parable of the suffering dependence that waits for God. Just as Jesus anticipated life with the Father in the shadow of the cross, so our elders minister to us with their hope in the face of inevitable decline and loss. In responding to them, we respond to the suffering Christ.

We admire those with spunk who stay on the move until they can move no more. Indeed, we should encourage those with youthful energy and strength to participate as full members of the community. Yet, we miss deep reserves of wisdom in our midst if we admire only those elderly people who look and act like younger adults. The hard work of living with limitations and losses plunges the aging person deeper into truth that sets us free.

Elderly people reminisce. They also complain. They move back and forth from the sublime to the ridiculous, griping about aching joints and bland food for one minute and remembering their crowning moment the next. Losing the armor of competence and independence embarrasses them and sometimes gets downright demeaning. Meanwhile, the search for the ultimate meaning of this life before it slips away can both exhilarate and exasperate.

Such are the throes of a worn-out body and mind giving birth to a soul. The older person must come full circle, become a child again, and spontaneously greet God when God appears before or after death. The elderly minister to us by letting us take care of them, and it is not necessarily their job to make it pretty any more than it is an infant's job to keep the diaper clean. They share with us this life on the edge called dying, a decline we younger adults face as well, only we have more props to help us deny it.

They show us our destiny in all its terror and beauty. In their suffering and deterioration, we see creation groaning in travail in anticipation of God's coming. In their gentleness, we see the peace that passes understanding.

The disciples attempted to turn the children away before Jesus intervened and named their ministry. We turn away from our elders all too often and distract ourselves with busyness like squirrels. As the sun rises and sets on this life, we cannot bear the terrible blaze of grace.

Thus, in the family discipline of caring for our elders, we live on the edge. Resurrection followed the cross. Just so, the view of God's face, the feel of God's loving hand, the freedom of living in God's kingdom often follow the long, monotonous days, the grinding struggles to do formerly simple things such as grocery shopping.

Yet, if we live wakefully, watching for the kingdom in the days of decline, we may see the kingdom amid the tasks of dying even before the death is done. Moreover, if our elder fulfills the vocation of dying well, we may see the kingdom in our midst in spite of ourselves.

My grandfather died at ninety-six in a retirement home. His daughter diligently cared for him through the hard final years as he suffered numerous strokes and grieved the death of his wife. I remember the small room in the infirmary that could not contain this former missionary and retired pastor as he diligently paid pastoral visits to his fellow patients.

Grandfather struggled terribly with the loss of his faculties, often bemoaning his sense of worthlessness. Yet, he found his calling like the hermits on Skellig Michael. He kept an old, black book listing missionaries all over the world. He spent hours each day in the antiseptic silence of his room praying for them—and for my aunt who cared for him along with those of us who visited him all too seldom. As the world rushed by down the busy street in front of the retirement home, this old man prayed for that world and for the ones with whom he shared the calling of ministry and the calling of family.[7]

Grace will not fail to touch this broken world as long as those who heed God's call to prayer at Skellig Michael or the retirement home infirmary lift up their hearts to God. God also calls us to prayer at home as we discipline the screaming child or love the tired spouse. Resurrection arises on the other side of death and waiting, and if we love each other enough to pray for each other, the kingdom will come at home as it does where saints pray in solitude.

QUESTIONS FOR REFLECTION AND DISCUSSION

1. Remember that a calling is not a job description, but a deeply personal challenge from God through which you find meaning and joy and address the world's needs. What is your calling in your family? How does your family calling bring you closer to God?

2. What demons have you or someone you love faced in family life? How have those demons obstructed or distorted your relationship with

God? How has God overcome those demons or used those demons to bring grace into your life?

3. Recall a time when you "saw the face of God" in an encounter with a family member. What did that event reveal about your calling? Share this story with a study group, a family member, or a trusted friend and ask for their feedback on its implications for your calling.

CHAPTER 12

The Politics of Everyday Life

DOING POLITICS

Wherever two or more gather, there is politics. Politics happens when people attempt to work out and implement a shared goal or vision. Our most basic political statements begin with "Let us" or "Let's." Let's go bowling. Let's finish this report by the end of the week. Let us end poverty and discrimination. Let's have a baby. Let us worship God. Whenever we make such statements through word or deed, we do politics.

Yet, we think political life only goes on in high places far from our humble homes, neighborhoods, and work places. We think of politicians as highly educated people in business suits who spend long hours in meetings telling lies and going to news conferences to depict their opponents as liars. At least the media portrays them that way. If they find true public servants in high places, media reporters would not tell us about them. It does not make good copy. This sad, cynical state of affairs diminishes all of us because we are all politicians.

All of us adopt a vision of the good life together, and all of us offer that vision to others in various ways, both subtle and obvious. We cannot do otherwise. When a co-worker asks us to lunch, our response says something about the kind of workplace we envision. When we attend (or fail to attend) a community meeting on recycling, we make a statement about the kind of environment we envision for all of us. When the pastor says, "Let us pray," and we bow our heads, we make a political statement about the relationship between our community and the same God to whom we pray in the privacy of our rooms.

Most of the politics that makes the news or break-room conversation involves conflict, and most of us think politics necessarily entails conflicting interests. So we do not care much for politics, especially if we do not like conflict. Conflict leads to coercion at worst or compromise at best, neither of which leaves anybody fully satisfied in the long run. When things do not go our way, we declare ourselves victims of politics. So we do not need to hear that politics is not always pretty. We know that.

What we need to hear is that politics is everywhere and that it blends in with the routine of our days. Conflict often accompanies politics, but does not define it. The essence of politics involves seeking common cause, not conflict. Yet, as unique individuals who bring different interests, different egos, and different visions of common cause to the table, we must deal with many conflicts in everyday politics. Nobody rises above that. We compromise and do things together all the time while taking the politics for granted.

Like it or not, we are all politicians, and we will not bring sanity to public life by waiting for professional politicians to work it out. Rather, we must mind our own political behavior. We must not try to live a spiritual life separate from our political life. We must take responsibility for our visions of common cause and how we put them on the table. We must take responsibility for our part in conflicts, how we use and abuse power, whether we live selfishly or unselfishly.

Once we take responsibility for our political life, we can cultivate a spirituality of politics, and we do not have to start from scratch. The Bible attests to God's constant activity in political life, from the high courts of David to the village well where a Jewish teacher discussed messianic hopes with a Samaritan woman. Jesus' teachings centered on the kingdom of God, and a kingdom is nothing if not political. We cannot separate spiritual life from political life because we cannot separate ourselves from the God of history who stirs our political world.

We typically use the term *community* to discuss the issues addressed in this chapter. Thus, the term *politics* may seem too narrow. Yet, the Bible compels me to use the less comfortable term *politics* because so many of the Bible's spiritual insights occur in a political context. The Bible tells about God's covenant relationship with a chosen nation and an adopted church. A covenant relationship entails a mutual agreement toward a common cause, so it is political through and through. The insights of

Genesis into faith and sin; the story of liberation and law in Exodus; the prophets' fierce spirituality; the exiled nation's hope; the Messiah's subversive victory over sin and death; the Holy Spirit's spread like wildfire through the Gentile world: All these biblical wonders unfold in the political context of our covenant relationship with God.

Without politics, we can sleep through our community life. Without politics, we can ignore the divine call to offer God our first fruits and to be our brothers' keeper. But to live wakefully in community life, we cannot avoid dedicating our political life to God.

POLITICS IN SURVIVAL MODE

When we introduced the three levels of wakefulness, we drew an analogy between the most basic level and the lives of squirrels, foraging for the winter and darting about to avoid every real or imaginary threat. We called this "survival mode," the mode in which most of us operate most of the time. In survival mode, we operate as if under siege, buttressing our fortifications, hoarding our goods, and preparing to protect what is ours.

In a capitalistic economy, another term we use for this mode of existence is "being realistic." We bless the pursuits of the self-interested individual, and we protect that individual's right to claim, accumulate, and defend property regardless of the needs of others. Yet, we fret little over the welfare of all because we place our faith in a providential "invisible hand" that takes care of the general welfare as long as everyone minds his or her own affairs. That is reality to us;

thus, we deem it "unrealistic" to question the individual's maximum pursuit of personal gain and security.

This approach seems to work better than any others. The communist experiment strove to move us beyond the squirrel level to the citizen level, devoting our economic lives to the welfare of the whole state, not of the self-interested individual. Yet, the self-interested individual conquered most communist nations. Self-interest made totalitarian leaders lose their cooperative vision in the quest for more personal power. Meanwhile, the rank and file grew lethargic in the absence of sufficient personal incentives.

Capitalism works because it refuses to challenge us spiritually as communism did. It refuses to require us to seek meaning beyond ourselves. A spiritual deadbeat can thrive materially without having to do the hard work of denying the self and caring for others. Marxists naively assumed that spiritual progress from the squirrel to the citizen level would occur spontaneously if we leveled the economic playing field. Capitalists bypassed that challenge by building a system that works just fine at the squirrel level.

So let us not recommend eliminating capitalism to make way for spiritual growth. Let us only acknowledge the profound challenge of living spiritually in a capitalistic economy. This economy programs us to think of everything in terms of a cost-benefit analysis. I had better buy flood insurance if I do not want to risk losing everything. I had better start eating more beta-carotene and less saturated fat if I want to live longer. I had better polish my resumé if I want to climb the corporate ladder. I had better not give too much to Save the Children or I might not save my own children. I had better play hardball with that contractor now or I might get a leaky roof later.

It's tough to turn off the cost-benefit din long enough to hear the still, small voice of God. It's tough to watch for signs of God's kingdom while I worry over the details of my kingdom. It's tough to put my heart and soul into statements that begin with "Let us" when I really want to say, "I want." It's tougher, Jesus said, for a rich person to enter the kingdom of God than it is for a camel to go through the eye of a needle (Luke 18:25).

Yet, Jesus offered some spiritual affirmations to our lives at the squirrel level. "Give us this day our daily bread," Jesus prayed for our survival. He offered our most basic needs up to God, and he invited us to say "I want" to God as a child might (Mark 10:15). He encouraged us to humbly acknowledge our most basic needs and trust God to care and take action on our behalf.

When it comes to our salvation, Jesus urged us not to be ashamed to seek the best we can get in the kingdom of God, even if we have to wheel and deal (Luke 16:1-13). Like a good capitalist, Jesus offered us a place in the kingdom that did not require us to give up our self-interest. Jesus spoke to our natural tendency to seek our own profit and gain, and he taught us how to maximize our profit in the kingdom. Yet, Jesus was too much of a capitalist for even us capitalists to bear because he said we must pay with our very lives for our greatest gain:

He called the crowd with his disciples, and said to them, "If any want to become my followers, let them deny themselves and take up their cross and follow me. For those who want to save their life will lose it, and those who lose their life for my sake, and for the sake of the gospel, will save it. For what will it profit them to gain the whole world and forfeit their life? Indeed, what can they give in return for their life?"

(Mark 8:34-37)

Obviously, Jesus calls us to a higher wakefulness than the squirrel level can maintain. He honors the squirrel level by telling us that God cares about our basic needs and by encouraging us to rely on God to meet them. Nevertheless, the squirrel level cannot get beyond the self; therefore, the squirrel level cannot suffice in the kingdom of God. We must look beyond ourselves, and that is the beginning of politics. Unless we look for a kingdom that brings joy to all in a community under God, we will not find it. We will only see our own dying reflection in a mirror dimly, never seeing face to face.

The Politics of Love

A scribe asked, "Which commandment is the first of all?" Jesus answered, "The first is, 'Hear, O Israel: the Lord our God, the Lord is one; you shall love the Lord your God with all your heart, and with all your soul, and with all your mind, and with all your strength'" (Mark 12:28-30). It seems that he did not consider the response complete until he answered the question: "Which is the second?" To this unspoken question, Jesus answered, "The second is this, 'You shall love your neighbor as yourself' " (v. 31). The scribe approved of Jesus' answer—a rarity for a scribe—and Jesus told him, "You are not far from the kingdom of God" (v. 34).

Love God. Love your neighbor. Believe that, live by that, and you are not far from the kingdom of God. Love of God and love of neighbor translates into the political statement at the heart of the kingdom: "Let us love one another" (1 John 4:7a).

Throughout the centuries of wedding liturgies and sentimental devotions, we have heard the command to love and have forgotten that it is political and therefore messy. More than messy—bloody, painful, terrifying. All one's heart, soul, mind, and strength this love of God demands. The love of neighbor—even of stranger, of enemy—demands one's very self.

In recent years, the person best known for her response to the command to love was Mother Teresa of Calcutta. At thirty- six, this Loreto nun responded to a call from God to give her life to loving the poorest of the poor on the streets of Calcutta, outside the window of the high school where she served as principal. For over a half century until her death in 1997, she ministered to the poor, the dying, the orphans, the lepers, the hopeless, the most marginalized people of the city.

In an interview with Sharon Gallagher, Mother Teresa revealed the beauty she found in the poor, "the kind of deep smile the poor have for each other in their families."[1] Only loving eyes can see such beauty, and she haunts us with the perception that we are the real poor, those of us who insulate ourselves in our air-conditioned homes, security systems, and employee benefits packages. This little wizened woman "with a dish towel on her head"[2] intimidates me. My everyday political life does not compare to hers, so sheltered am I in my middle-class, educated, employed, professional world with all its protective claims and norms.

She makes it no easier for me with her concluding words of the interview in which she alludes to Jesus' parable of the sheep and the goats in Matthew 25. "The poor are very beautiful people. We will be judged by what we have done to the poor, by what Christ has said. That if we saw them hungry, sick, naked, or in prison and didn't take them in, we will be judged as treating him in the way we have treated the poor."[3]

Her political statement seems to be, *Let us follow Christ and love the unloved and unlovely*. In stricter terms she seems to say, *Let us love the poorest of the poor*. Even more challenging, she says of herself and her co-workers with the poor, "We choose to be poor, because to understand the poor you must live a life of poverty."[4]

At first I feel very far from such a life of love. I fall very far short of this standard of self-sacrificial love. Moreover, I fall physically far from the poorest of the poor. I have arranged my daily life at work and at home so that I encounter them very little.

Will God let me succeed in fleeing from the poor? If so, the Father would let me flee far from his Son who enters our lives among the poor. But God does not let us escape the call to love the poor any more than God let Jonah get away.

Mother Teresa seems to say that the poor are always near us, that we may delude ourselves into thinking that we insulate ourselves from them, but we meet them daily. Her ministry began with the poor outside her window, at her doorstep. We can meet the poor with very small steps.

Mother Teresa recommends that we go no farther than our own family to begin living the political life of love:

> Love and concern begin at home. Then naturally, not by force, they will go out. But we don't know our own family unless we are awakened and that's how we can see poverty. It's easy to get involved in something far away, to send money. But that's not what they need. They don't need pity. If homes are all right, the world will be all right. Jesus tells us to love our neighbor, not the whole world—"as I have loved you," "as the Father has loved me." So the circle is completed.[5]

God calls us first to love the ones placed before us, our spouses and children, our co-workers and clients, the people on our daily paths, not an abstract "whole world" of our imagining. In calling us to love one another, Jesus issues a very humble call to love the people in our midst, not to become saviors of the world. If we start with the concrete needs closest to us, God will expand the boundaries of our love to the stranger and to the hungry and oppressed in faraway places. Our love for them will become as natural as our love for our children.

"The real poverty in the world today is loneliness,"[6] Mother Teresa contends, and I can understand that well from behind the layers of insulation I constructed. Yet, I can start there with my own poverty and love the lonely in my midst. Mother Teresa assures me that if I do, Jesus will peel away the insulation in which I wrapped my world. He will lead me to the poor whom he calls me to serve just as he led her to the poor of Calcutta outside her window.

Obviously, Mother Teresa took the first great commandment to love God with all her being as seriously as she took the second commandment to love her neighbor as herself. Yet, she came to the world's attention primarily for her adherence to the second commandment. She did not receive the Nobel Peace Prize for her devotion to God but for her work among the poor. An atheist can applaud her winning the prize as well-deserved while writing off her devotion to God as an archaic quirk.

In the midst of this struggle, we can easily forget the first commandment and focus on the second: Love your neighbor as yourself. We can forget God, even reject God and do that. Politics then becomes the business of loving one another all by ourselves, with no God to complicate this already complicated business of hammering out "let us" statements that we can say together and hold each other accountable to.

If we love without God, then all we need is democracy. It beats totalitarianism or dictatorship or fascism. Everybody has a vote. Everybody has a voice. Everybody can find somebody who comes close to wanting the same kind of life, the same kind of justice, the same kind of peace. Everybody can try to persuade everybody else, and if one's cause happens to be serving the poor, one can feel free to state that case in the public square.

Conventional secular wisdom recommends that if one holds that political agenda, do not quote Jesus. Better to keep faith and politics separate, surviving on their own power. After all, religion and the state litter history with their abuses of each other. So people devoted to just causes—saving the whale, feeding the hungry, sheltering the homeless, empowering the powerless—often embrace their causes in spite of rather than because of religion.

Such conventional wisdom has its merit. We must play by the rules of democracy, and we may form alliances with those who do not share our faith. Yet, we hide our light under a bushel if we keep quiet about the God who calls us and moves us and loves us.

Those who remember the first commandment to love God, those who remember that Jesus claimed to forever encounter us amidst suffering, those who believe that "Love is from God" (1 John 4:7) see signs of the kingdom amid the conflict and cooperation of their political lives. They see the face of God among the faces of ally and opponent alike. The God who sends them into the political dealings of their daily lives always meets them there.

That does not mean that the political life of wakeful Christians has any more harmony, sweetness, and light than anyone else's political life. In fact, Jesus cautioned us of much suffering in store. He warned that we must "be wise as serpents and innocent as doves" in the political environment of this world (Matthew 10:16). Reinhold Niebuhr counseled us to face the fact that we have some measure of power in politics, that we must seek God's guidance in exercising it, but that as sinners we will inevitably hurt somebody in the process.[7] That applies as much to the mundane affairs of our daily lives as it does to the business conducted on Capitol Hill.

So we blend in with the rest, slugging it out for power. Yet, we must keep the struggle from becoming our religion. We must keep from seeking power for power's sake. Those who enter the struggle for just causes in grateful obedience to God have a distinct mindfulness of Jesus, who reminds us of our own poverty and makes us mindful of the call to love others in their poverty rather than to hoard power for ourselves.

We inevitably fall short, of course. None of us can say we fully heed the first commandment to love God, because none of us love each other with anything near the love God gave through the Son (1 John 4:20). So we must seek a higher way still in our political lives. We must set aside our political agendas and patiently, attentively discern God's political agenda. We must seek the kingdom of God.

THE POLITICS OF THE KINGDOM

Jesus taught us to pray, "Thy kingdom come," and in teaching that, Jesus did politics of the highest order. "Thy kingdom come" implies the following political statements: Let us set aside our personal visions of the common good and seek God's vision for the common good. Let us put faith not in our programs but in God's program. Let us not assume that we hold God's program in our grasp, that our programs are God's. Let us humbly seek to discern day by day God's will for us as communities, as nations, as one world. Let us pray that God will use our fallible works and programs for purposes beyond our purposes, for wonders beyond our ideals.

Praying "Thy kingdom come" has enormous political consequences. It implies that no political party is God's party. It leaves no room for an "old time religion of conservative politics" as a senator from Mississippi once proclaimed. It allows no liberal party to offer good news to the poor and marginalized that comes close to God's good news to them. Political life at the highest level of wakefulness entails standing at a distance from all human parties and persuasions and casting the critical eye of a prophet on them.

A prophetic approach to politics recognizes that those who identify a party or ideology with the gospel fail to worship God. The walls of a temple, the borders of a nation, the interests of a class cannot confine God whose love always bursts like raging waters through the dams we erect to contain and keep it. The identification of one political party or ideology with God's will reduces religion to idolatry and politics to bigotry.

God is free and jealous. God demands our allegiance first, then we must look to political parties as limited, ephemeral vehicles to seek and speak God's will in the public square. The prophetic challenge to live our political lives in true worship of the one God will outlive our political parties and ideologies.[8]

The biblical prophets have some deeper lessons to teach us about the spirituality of political life. Samuel convicted King Saul of leading the people without waiting for God, with doing things the most practical way instead of leading the people in doing things the most holy way. Nathan found King David guilty of acting like a lord over his subjects' lives rather than remembering that God cherishes the life and dignity of every citizen. Amos and Micah indicted the people of Israel for using rituals of worship in the temple to manipulate God rather than worshiping God through loving the poor, the vulnerable, the stranger on the streets. Isaiah of Jerusalem accused the king of trusting power politics rather than the mysterious work of God in political affairs. Jeremiah convicted the people of Judah for complacently taking God for granted rather than entering into an authentic relationship with their Lord.

The Hebrew prophets' fundamental indictment of everyday politics in Israel and Judah came to this: You do not worship God in your political affairs. You delude yourselves into thinking that you do, but you do not. In contemporary America, the indictments would sound something like this: Your forefathers and mothers came here to worship God freely, but you place your trust in the security of fighter planes, mutual funds, and computer chips. You work hard, vote, and go to church, but you conceal your breaking heart from God. You love your family and the people in your community who look like you and act like you, but in ignoring or rejecting the stranger, you fail to worship the God who came as a stranger. In putting the poor and disadvantaged at the bottom of your list of political priorities, you fail to worship the God who was reviled and spit upon and beaten. In your success at making good appearances, you do not know what to do with the crucified God.

Political life from a prophetic perspective, therefore, always begins with repentance. The withering charge of the prophets gets us every time, and we cannot live politically in God's kingdom until we plead guilty and submit ourselves to the judge. The judge loves us and wants us to be free, so he frees us to worship God in our community life each day.

From the prophetic perspective, our "let us" statements must always begin with confession. Talk radio hosts and the cynics next door pollute our air with self-righteous charges against those who harbor a different vision, but the critics invariably forget to confess their own political sins. Thus, they forget to worship God.

What does a political life of worship look like on weekdays? What does it look like between election days? How do we identify political saints on the streets, the ones who do not necessarily make the news or the papers, the ones whom we may emulate? We must find an answer, for otherwise we cannot see the kingdom flourishing in the nooks and crannies of our days. Jesus showed us in the upper room as he washed his disciples' feet. He showed us as he gave them bread and wine and told them to consider that his very self which he gives them to take into their bloodstream and to give them life. He showed us as he offered their lives with his to God in prayer.

Disciples worship God quietly, almost invisibly on the streets and in the houses of commerce and over the phone wires. They seek out opportunities to honor the last as the first. They treat the telemarketer with courtesy, befriend the stranger in the cafe, listen to the complainer with patience. They go to their children's tee-ball games, march to raise money for AIDS victims, and go out of their way to make sure a co-worker gets the credit she deserves. They write their senator on behalf of oppressed people half a world away whose welfare will win no votes and will gain us no national security.

These seem commonplace deeds of good will. Many persons do them only because they are good folks, nice people. Nevertheless, wakeful ones do them in remembrance of the One who interrupts us, who comes as One unknown on the road, who has no decent place of his own to lay his head. Wakeful ones see in such small acts of unobtrusive worship the mustard seeds that God nurtures into great trees, the conquests over evil that God uses to clear the way for the kingdom's coming.

Wakeful ones know that the legislators and executives and judges of this world depend on such seemingly insignificant acts. They depend on such acts in part because their programs and structures will collapse without the foundation of public civility. Yet even more so, they depend on such acts because this is God's world, not theirs, and their reign has no meaning without God's reign.

The kingdom is as vital and unseen as our worshiping hearts. Yet, the kingdom does not rise and fall with our hearts. The kingdom originates in the heart of Christ. "Let us love one another," he calls through an apostle. "Let us worship God," he calls through the preacher. With those calls, our Lord begins the politics of each day, and with those calls God will end politics on the final day.

QUESTIONS FOR REFLECTION AND DISCUSSION

1. Consider three recent occasions in which you explicitly or implicitly addressed someone with a statement beginning with "Let us." (Trivial requests count.) What did each statement imply about the kind of relationship you want to have with the people (or person) you addressed? What did it imply about the kind of community you envision?

2. Choose the word you prefer: "liberal" or "conservative." (Choose one. "Moderate" is not allowed.) Outline or write, from a Christian perspective, a one page defense of the term you *did not* choose. What did this exercise reveal about the limitations of the position you prefer?

3. Mother Teresa's critics claimed that she would have done the sick and dying poor a greater service by working to change the political injustices that led to their plight rather than limiting her ministry to compassionate care. How would you defend her? Does this criticism reveal some shortcomings of the political spirituality presented here?

CHAPTER 13

Wasting Time

DOXOLOGY

A doxology is a song of praise to God. Moreover, doxologies do nothing more than praise God. A single-minded song, doxology does not mean praise plus petition, praise plus complaint, or even praise plus thanksgiving. It means praise, period. Doxology boldly implies that praise is sufficient.

I can mark my maturation by what doxology meant to me through the years. The refrain, "Praise God, from whom all blessings flow; / praise him, all creatures here below; / praise him above, ye heavenly host; / praise Father, Son, and Holy Ghost," will remain indelibly etched in my brain forever. We Presbyterians usually sing it after the offering.

As a child, I sang it lazily as we watched the ushers march back up the center aisle with the brass plates full of white envelopes, dollar bills, and pocket change—including the quarters that my Dad gave me to put in. Grown-ups seemed quite reverent about money, so the combination of money, organ music, and words praising God "above, ye heavenly hosts" carried a reverence that seemed too adult for me to participate in. When I sang the doxology, I felt like I was doing something sneaky, like taking Communion before I was old enough. Yet, nobody seemed to mind.

After communicants' class, when I could take Communion, I noticed that the doxology included praises to God "from whom all blessings flow." As the ushers took the collection plates to the waiting minister, I put two and two together. In the doxology, we really thank God, giving our gifts and acknowledging God as the source of all good gifts, including the checks and dollars and quarters in the brass plates. For some eloquent reason, we do not come right out and say, "Thank you." Maybe we are a living, singing word of thanks ourselves.

I suppose I could have gone the rest of my life with that point of view, but as I entered middle age, I grew skeptical. The doxology *does not* say "thank you." It says "praise God." Period. It acknowledges no practical program, no reciprocal exchange, no means to any ends. It is an end in itself. The doxology is worth singing regardless of whether or how much we put in the collection plate and regardless of whether and how much we feel blessed by God. God inspires praise. We "creatures here below" cannot help singing.

I have not finished growing up. I can only speculate about what the doxology will come to mean next. Perhaps I will go full circle, and it will come to mean again what it meant to me as a child. A song over my head, a reverence too great for my heart. Something for angels to sing, not a little one like me with his feet on the ground and dirt in his nails. I will feel unworthy to sing it, graced but lost in the scandal of my singing while no one seems to object.

Opportunities for doxology come each day for those awake enough to seize them. The opportunities often come in the form of time to waste, time that can come by accident or by design. At such times we can forget making our time count for profit or personal growth or home improvement. Such opportunities offer therapy for those driven by work or domestic responsibilities, but for the wakeful, their therapeutic value seems trivial before the glowing light of God's glory. While we cannot exhaust the many ways God offers us daily chances for doxology, we will examine those opportunities in the forms of Sabbath, play, and sleep.

SABBATH

Abraham Joshua Heschel congratulated us technologically sophisticated moderns for our conquest of space. We isolated the DNA molecule and walked on the moon. We packed volumes of data and powers of calculation into fingernail-sized chips, and we developed communication networks that span from our living rooms to other continents via orbiting satellites. We split the atom, and in so doing, we harnessed the power to destroy the planet many times over. We manipulated our blood chemistry to ward off plagues, and we reshaped the landscape with our highways and wires and factories and cities. We manipulated things in space seemingly unimpeded.

But the clock ticks as always. We cannot speed it up or slow it down without making it a liar. The earth orbits the sun, our final spatial marker for the passing of the days, but it is only a marker. Time has its own integrity. We cannot touch it. Albert Einstein identified time's influence over the dynamics of space, but he never dared speak of manipulating it. In the death of each person, time swallows space, and all our conquests come to dust, all our frontiers to darkness.

Thus, Heschel argues, those who approach time with appropriate humility and reverence will find holiness there. They will find the mark of the one God who created space as our playground and time as our destiny. God lovingly gave us the Sabbath as a time to set aside our struggle for temporary mastery over space and share in the eternal bounty of time.[1]

> Remember the Sabbath day by keeping it holy. Six days you shall labor and do all your work, but the seventh day is a Sabbath to the LORD your God. On it you shall not do any work, neither you, nor your son or daughter, nor your manservant or maidservant, nor your animals, nor the alien within your gates. For in six days the LORD made the heavens and the earth, the sea, and all that is in them, but he rested on the seventh day. Therefore the LORD blessed the Sabbath day and made it holy.
>
> (Exodus 20:8-11, NIV)

Keep the Sabbath holy, God commands, and in doing so God bids us set the day apart. We must see God's mark in it, the prints of the divine fingers that shaped us and the spatial world in which we labor through the week. We accept this gift of time.

"The sabbath was made for humankind, and not humankind for the sabbath; so the Son of Man is lord even of the sabbath" (Mark 2:27). Jesus said this to Pharisees browbeating him for allowing his disciples to pluck grain for food on the Sabbath. The Pharisees forgot the Sabbath was a gift and made it an oppressive requirement. As the disciples munched behind him, Jesus reminded the self-appointed guardians of holiness before him that holiness starts with the grateful acceptance of a gift, not with the compulsive earning of a trifle.

We lost Sabbath observance in America because we equated the grateful acceptance of a gift with doing what we please. Jesus' defense of his disciples means to us, "Let them do what they want. The Sabbath was made for them, not them for the Sabbath." Yet, we lost Sabbath observance because we do not know very well what we want. We want somebody to tell us what we want. We might even welcome Pharisees in our lives to tell us how to spend our Sabbaths, and some of us find them.

Yet, most of us, lacking Pharisees, take our guidance from the most easily accessible authorities. The television tells us to watch football, drink beer, and covet cars, so we do. The work ethic that drove us through the week gladly continues to drive us, so we catch up on housework or yard work or even go back to the office. Even church becomes a surrogate work place for many where we labor in committee meetings and program implementation. We let the work ethic and the leisure culture rob us of our

Sabbath because we never really decided for ourselves to accept God's blessing of time as a holy gift.

This is not a call for the return of Sabbath laws and for all the stores to close on Sundays. Our civil society has no official religion, nor should it. Perhaps the ancient nomads could better manage consecrating every seventh day better than industrialized moderns. But unless we make significant time for resting in God we will reach the end of our days without awakening to the holiness that dwells uniquely in time. We will conquer space without time's blessing until at last time conquers us.

The commandment to observe the Sabbath underscores an irony. Sabbath time is our most precious gift. Yet, it takes terrific discipline to hold it and cherish it. Observing the Sabbath requires the discipline of making time to honor the loving God by accepting the rest that God offers now, not sometime in the distant future after one makes a million dollars or puts in forty-five good years for the company. It requires time for intimacy with God, the time we long for so deeply that we scarcely allow ourselves to acknowledge it.

Sometimes I doubt that I can handle this discipline, so easily do the pressures of work, competition, or escape seduce me. Perhaps Sabbath observance needs more than personal discipline. Perhaps it needs grace.

Such grace comes in the form of interruptions—the traffic jam on the way home from work, the phone call from someone who confounds my driven work routine by asking how I am doing, the lights going out just as I settle in front of the television. Interruptions shatter the delusion that I control and manage "my" time. They provide opportunities to pray or love.

Prayer and love: Those are the things we really want to do. Wakeful discipline seizes those opportunities when grace surprises us.

Observing the Sabbath in this age subverts everything. It takes God seriously in a world embarrassed by God. We spend time on God despite the world's loud insistence that time is money and that God helps those who help themselves. A few who observe the Sabbath often start making time for God after hitting bottom, like the recovering alcoholic who makes frequent times for meetings and devotions. Some observe the Sabbath because they cannot forget the sweetness of scripture study and prayer. Others go about their business not looking forward to another conquest in space but remembering and anticipating the eternity revealed in Sabbath times.

Such saints know what they want to do and do it. They know what all of us want to do, and they do it for us. No wealth or accomplishment ever brought such contentment or privilege as that.

PLAY

In Sabbath time, we honor God. In play, we celebrate God's blessings.

Like doxology, play serves no useful purpose. We play for the sake of play, for the enjoyment inherent in it. Additional agendas corrupt play. If I play tennis not only for joy of playing but for the satisfaction of beating the other guy and for the exercise that might help deter a heart attack, I lost the spirit of play before I started.

Play differs from doxology because the latter explicitly and intentionally praises God while play implicitly and unconsciously praises God by enjoying God's gifts. The gifts include health, mobility, skill, fresh air, laughter, and the like. Our play praises God when we lose ourselves like children in the enjoyment of these gifts.

Despite the tremendous sums of time and money we invest in sports and recreation, adults scarcely engage in true play. We work hard at play, packing in so many additional agendas that it exhausts us. Our play takes planning and packing and charge cards and practice, practice, practice. On our vacations, we anxiously seek optimum experiences: breathtaking views, sunny skies, the best wine and food, the most upscale entertainment. Our anxious pursuit of the best never abates from the time we leave the office to the time we return.

Perhaps that is just reality on this side of Eden. Perhaps that is our lot in life. Just as we seldom love without the contamination of selfish motives, so we seldom engage in unadulterated play. Yet, just as we love best by acknowledging our selfish motives and keeping them in check, so we must do with play. Only at our peril do we resign ourselves to the agendas that latch onto play like leeches. We may have great vacations and terrific tennis matches without having much fun in the end.

My dog knows how to play. I take her to her yard, and she runs for a stray tennis ball. She retrieves it and prances toward me proudly displaying her catch, growling out her power. Then she plays "keep away," showing me the ball and pulling it back, shaking her head like a lion. Finally, she lets me get my hand on it, but not after a few evasions on her part and clever, clumsy footwork on mine. She plays tug-of-war. Sometimes she wins, but more often she lets me have the ball, and I throw it. She retrieves it, and the cat-and-mouse game begins again.

I usually have something else to do or someplace else to go when she challenges me to this sport, but I cannot refuse her wide-eyed excitement. Her initiation of this game interrupts me, makes me forget my goals and pressing tasks for a few minutes until she gets distracted and the game ends. Through my dog, Katie, God interrupts my day with Sabbath time, a time to enjoy our Creator's blessings through play, a time to enjoy being a creature with Katie.

Our children, of course, minister to us in the same way if we let them. Their naiveté about our pressing tasks blesses us, helps us put our anxieties in perspective. Sit on the floor and play with blocks or follow the drama of a family of dolls. Our children teach us much in those times about what is important. We learn how to love them in their make-believe worlds and towering construction projects, and likewise they learn there on the floor that we love them. Thus, they fulfill their calling, their vocation, and through them God calls us to the Sabbath time of play with a compelling small voice.

SLEEP

This book started with the question, "Why do we get up in the morning?" Now before we conclude, let us ask, "Why do we go to bed at night?"

As of this writing, scientists do not know the answer to that question. They have a few theories: Perhaps we go to bed at night to allow our body to make repairs. Perhaps we need the insanity of our dreams lest we go crazy by day. Perhaps we need to shut off our conscious minds to allow our unconscious minds to process all of the day's input. Nobody has the hard medical or psychological data to nail down the final answer to *why* we need sleep.

Yet, we do not need to wait for the scientists to tell us *that* we do need it. The bleary-eyed, sluggish feeling at the end of a long day tells us all we need to know. When the scientific answer finally arrives, sleep will still seem shrouded in mystery. At the end of the day, we voluntarily strip ourselves, recline, and give up consciousness—quite a reversal from our day-long struggles to control our time and our children and our cash flow. At the end of the night, we come to and, if we sleep well, we wonder how the time passed unnoticed.

The physiological answer to the question, "Why do we go to bed at night?" may come in time, but sleep has its place in the spiritual life as well. Just as sleep plays a crucial part in preparing our bodies for wakefulness, it also serves a crucial function in the wakefulness of our faith. Some locate this function in our dreams.

My wife remembers her dreams and usually has a report in the morning of the kindness or cruelty that her friends or family members or co-workers or I showed in them. In her dreams she moves from peril to peace and back again. I seldom remember my dreams, but I know I have them. I often awaken with the strange feeling that I will never be the same again, almost like Jesus' father Joseph who could scarcely sleep without an angel visiting with news about his son, the Messiah.

For some people, dreams provide a rich text for spiritual self-understanding. Dreams help them tap into realities beyond those we perceive in waking, and the analysis of dreams becomes a virtual spiritual exercise that helps them to see their lives anew when awake. Such persons often turn to Carl Jung or one of his disciples for guidance.[2]

I see the awareness of one's dream life and the ability to find meaning in it as a spiritual gift, but not as a necessity to wakeful faith. If the reader finds that gift useful, see the works of one of the authors noted above. When considering the spiritual significance of sleep, the voluntary entrance into vulnerable unconsciousness fascinates me more. The trust all of us muster up amazes me. Sleep supports spiritual wakefulness as a radical exercise in the trust so essential to faith.

"It is in vain that you rise up early and go late to rest, eating the bread of anxious toil; for he provides for his beloved during sleep"(Psalm 127:2; see footnote in NRSV). That feeling I have upon awakening that I will never be the same again may have less to do with my dreams than they have to do with God's work in my life while I slept. Maybe dreams long since forgotten gave intimations of God's work in my life, or maybe not. Sleep is shrouded in mystery, yes, the mystery not of my psyche, but of God's gracious work.

When I go to bed at night, I implicitly accept that mystery, a mystery that includes the question with which I awakened: Why do I get up in the morning? What is the meaning of my life? I never go to bed with the answer quite complete. Maybe I need tomorrow to help me answer it. Maybe I need a night's sleep.

Maybe I need death and a God who has conquered death. As a child, I ended each day with the prayer: "Now I lay me down to sleep, I pray the Lord my soul to keep. If I should die before I wake, I pray the Lord my soul to take." In retrospect, it seems incredible that so many millions of children find comfort in thoughts of death just before sleeping. Yet, in sleeping we make peace daily with death. We play at giving up the ghost, letting our consciousness go, reclining our bodies in utter vulnerability, and seeing our souls off to a mysterious realm. We end each day like that, however vague the outcomes of our day's activities may seem.

In chapter 1, I discussed the transitions to higher levels of wakefulness as responses to a greater awareness of death. The squirrel level becomes inadequate to us in proportion to our awareness that death makes our scurrying to survive futile. So we move on to the citizen level, finding meaning in relationships and communities, only to face the reality that we die alone. This calls us to higher wakefulness, voluntarily dying to the search for our own fulfillment and finding our joy and meaning in God alone.

Higher wakefulness gives us peace with death because it embraces mystery. At the end of each day, we go to bed with many unanswered questions, much unfinished business. Will today's mistakes catch up with me tomorrow? Will those who make promises today keep them tomorrow? Will my child, my spouse, my soul make it through the night and another day without calamity? Will the seeds sown today ever bear fruit? When we go to sleep, we let go of those questions consciously while our unconscious minds turn them over. We forget ourselves, give it all up in faith to the mystery of God's plan.

So it is with higher wakefulness, and so it is with death. We die with the meaning of our lives still not fully realized, like Moses viewing the promised land from afar and then giving up the ghost. The meaning of our lives is beyond us, and we go to sleep at night and face our death with the faith that it is working itself out in loving hands. In wakeful living, we go to sleep at night looking forward to intimations of that meaning tomorrow. In wakeful dying, we depart with the same hope after a lifetime of nightly practice.

QUESTIONS FOR REFLECTION AND DISCUSSION

1. Imagine that you attempt to set aside one full day this week for Sabbath observance. What changes and hard choices will you make to set aside the time? What would you do on that day? What rewards would you gain?

2. In the section on play, I discussed my dog, Katie, and how she engages me in play. Think of a person or pet who does or did the same for you. Describe your play together. What blessings did your playful companion celebrate in the playing?

3. Before going to bed tonight, write down three unanswered questions about your life. Pray for

God's help with each question. Then put the questions in an envelope and go to bed. Review the questions again in the morning, and consider this: What has God disclosed to you about those questions in the night? What remains unanswered? Pray again for the questions, and return to them whenever you wish during the day or the week to come. Take notes on how you perceive God guiding you with those questions. How does God's guidance as you sleep compare to God's guidance while you are awake?

PART III

concluding Questions

CHAPTER 14

Wakefulness, Suffering, and Heavenly Hopes

I work at a college. Despite my earlier years earning a doctorate, I serve not in the ivory tower offices of the faculty, but in the counselor's office. Sometimes I envy the faculty for their status, their time to write and do research, their stimulating interactions in class. More often, however, I cherish my special intimacy with students who share their struggles and milestones both dire and mundane.

Rather than working in other settings that need psychologists, I chose to practice my profession in higher education in part because colleges and universities serve as society's institutional guardians of doubt. In medical settings, businesses, government agencies, and churches, "I don't know," usually does not cut it as an answer to the burning question of the day. It does not get us any closer to the institution's particular bottom line. Not so in college classrooms: Doubt is the negative charge in the magnetic field of learning. The truth has no draw without it.

I enjoy the richness of sharing with students their struggles as the doubts and affirmations of classroom experiences blend with the anxieties and delights of becoming adults. Moreover, I work at a college that places religion at the heart of its mission. That affords an ethos of freedom to discuss matters of faith alongside the struggles of surviving organic chemistry, coming to terms with sexual abuse, or dealing with shyness.

Faith and doubt generate their electricity in my office on a daily basis. I feel the static still as I write this book. I hear the words of doubt (both mine and the students') as I write, and in conclusion, I wish to address some of those doubts that still draw me to the search for spiritual truth.

One crucial doubt concerns the question, "When will the rewards of wakefulness come?" If I answer, "Now," then why do the faithful still suffer depression, heartache, anxiety, and loss like everyone else? That question has a face. It issues from a tall young sophomore woman who majors in business. Bible verses adorn her tee-shirt and a pewter sign of the fish dangles at the end of her necklace. Mascara stains her cheeks, tears from the struggle to understand her depression that seemed to come from nowhere. She pulls back her long red hair and waits for an answer.

On the other hand, if I answer, "Later, in heaven," to the question of when the faithful will receive their satisfaction, then is faith just a delusional escape from the responsibilities and sufferings of this life? That question too has a face. It issues from a junior pre-med student with a 4.0 average who calls himself an agnostic. He wears a baseball cap that shields his downcast eyes. He clenches fist and jaw alternately as he works through rage at his estranged father who smothered him with condemning Bible verses, then left his mother when no one was looking. The bill of the cap lifts, revealing deep brown eyes that pierce me in search of an answer.

In the final pages of this book, I will address those students' questions as well as I can in the two-dimensional world of the printed page. Of course, in the real world, they will find their answers in the trials and joys of their lives that they must live as works of art. I cannot prescribe the colors, times, or places for their answers, and I cannot for you, the reader. Yet, I hope the following discussion offers something useful for the interplay of affirmation and doubt and for the wakefulness of our .faith.

Now

In the previous chapters, I emphasized the rewards of faithfulness in the present. That has been the main thrust of the book. When Jesus calls us to be awake, he calls us not to postpone life until his return or until heavenly bliss after death, but he calls us to heed the signs of the kingdom in our midst, the face of God among us. As I wrote the chapters above, the young man with the angry eyes under a baseball cap sat before me the whole time, glaring. I wanted to answer his skepticism about our motives. I wanted him to know that through faith, God calls us to greater responsibility for our present life precisely because we cannot otherwise realize the joy that God promises to the faithful.

Yet, the young woman visited me more and more as the chapters unfolded. "Why should I desire wakefulness," she asked, "unless it overcomes all my unhappiness?" She reminded me how worship and

Bible studies and songs and prayers do not totally erase her unhappiness. She really made me squirm when she reminded me of my unhappiness—the self-doubts of mid-life, the stress of overwork, grief that will not go away, days at work when everything seems to go wrong. How can I write so confidently of wakefulness when she and I still suffer in our various miserable ways?

She asks an ancient question. She asks it from this campus, full of trees, wide open spaces, and grand old buildings full of history and tradition. This place seems so safe, so removed from the "real world." Many visit here and wonder how such a place could need a counselor, how anyone could have problems here.

Yet, on this side of Eden, the demons of our yesterdays and the dragons of our futures rage at the edge of such places. She knows this well, my faithful young questioner. She hears the cries of the demons from her young but very long past. She feels the earth shake from the dragons stalking recklessly through her tomorrows.

The prophet Habakkuk also stood in a pristine place, listening to the violence at its borders. Jerusalem's sinful yesterdays filled the air with howling, cackling demons, and the earth trembled with the hooves of tomorrow's dragons drawing near the gates. The mighty Chaldeans harassed Jerusalem, toying with it before the kill. In this place and time of impending doom, Habakkuk offered a variant of my young friend's question to God:

> O LORD, how long shall I cry for help,
>   and you will not listen?

Or cry to you "Violence!"
    and you will not save?
Why do you make me see wrong-doing
    and look at trouble?
Destruction and violence are before me;
    strife and contention arise.
So the law becomes slack
    and justice never prevails.
The wicked surround the righteous—
    therefore judgment comes forth perverted.
                    (Habakkuk 1:2-4)

Why do the faithful and righteous suffer? Why stay awake for a God who sends such terror? Does wakeful watchfulness change the indifferent course of the demons and dragons that torment us?

Habakkuk did not wait for logic or inspiration to give him the answer. He took action based on the preposterous hope that wakeful watchfulness changes things. The prophet watched for God's face, waited for God to answer:

I will stand at my watchpost,
    and station myself on the rampart;
I will keep watch to see what he will say to me,
    and what he will answer concerning my
complaint.
Then the LORD answered me and said:
    Write the vision;
    make it plain on tablets,
    so that a runner may read it.
For there is still a vision for the appointed time;
    it speaks of the end, and does not lie.

If it seems to tarry, wait for it;
 it will surely come, it will not delay.
Look at the proud!
 Their spirit is not right in them,
 but the righteous live by their faith.
          (Habakkuk 2:1-4)

Watch. Wait. The humble will receive their justice. The righteous live in the meantime by faith. Faith itself will be their reward. Waiting will have its own consolations if done in watchfulness, in confident anticipation. The faithful will know a deeper justice, a joy that springs not from having worldly power or the favor of fate, but from being right with God and having a friendly relationship with the Lord.

As a student in another pristine place, I heard the demons and dragons in the background while I listened to a lecture on Habakkuk's words. My Old Testament professor said that Habakkuk did not mean that the righteous live by faith in some future life. The ancient Hebrews did not yet have a concept of heavenly bliss. Habakkuk meant that the righteous live by faith now, in this life, even with the Chaldeans breathing down their necks.

Even if one believes in the afterlife, faith does not require the rewards of heavenly bliss to console us. Faith offers satisfaction sufficient for today. Faith is not antidepressant medication, soothing and leveling our moods. It is not magic, exorcising our demons and slaying our dragons with the wave of a wand. It does not make life fair, and it does not render us immune to suffering. At times it makes us vulnerable to suffering, to taking up our crosses. It does not serve as a means to any other end because it is the end. Faith is its own reward even today, and for those who watch and wait, suffering increases faith.

Habakkuk closed his short book with a prayer, and in the final verses the reader knows that this prophet prayed not only with eloquent words but with listening ears. He clearly heard a consolation that only God can give to faith, and the prophet offered it back in praise:

> Though the fig tree does not blossom,
> and no fruit is on the vines;
> though the produce of the olive fails
> and the fields yield no food;
> though the flock is cut off from the fold
> and there is no herd in the stalls,
> yet I will rejoice in the LORD;
> I will exult in the God of my
> salvation.
> GOD, the Lord, is my strength;
> he makes my feet like the feet
> of a deer,
> and makes me tread upon the
> heights.
>
> (Habakkuk 3:17-19)

If "faith is the assurance of things hoped for, the conviction of things not seen" (Hebrews 11:1), more than physical invisibility blocks those precious things from our sight. Faith is the conviction of things not seen because we see so much suffering and injustice that we can hardly imagine the fulfillment of God's promises. Faith is the assurance of things hoped for although the reality we live in seems so far beyond hope. In faith, we hunger and thirst for meaning and purpose despite all the disappointments and doubts of our lives, and we hold the long suffering hope that the meaning and purpose of our daily lives rest in loving hands.

The consolations and rewards of faith make no sense apart from the mundane, concrete reality of our daily lives. They make no sense apart from my young client's routine of study, her problems with a demanding roommate, her hopes for a letter from home in her mail box. Faith enables her to face her depression and work her way straight through it rather than around, over, or under it. She heads in the right direction as she sits before me with tears streaming down her cheeks and Kleenex balled up in her clutching hands. And God goes with her.

LATER, IN HEAVEN

Faith is its own reward, even today amidst suffering. That statement really answers both of my questioners. To the young woman who questions faith that does not protect her from suffering, that statement offers faith as the one joy deep enough not only to withstand any anguish but to grow stronger in suffering. To the young man who questions the authenticity of faith, caricaturing it as an otherworldly escape from the responsibility of living today, we offer faith as a reward thoroughly grounded in the present and in the problems of daily living.

Yet, shall we deny any answer tomorrow? Shall we join my agnostic friend in snubbing hope for heaven as wishful thinking, a failure to take death seriously? Hope for heaven certainly can keep many of us at a squirrel level of spiritual growth, scurrying about to do good deeds and to watch our language so we can cash in on judgment day. Or it can keep us so caught up in dreams of meeting an ethereal Jesus in heaven that we distract ourselves from his flesh and blood presence in the suffering around us. Such immature forms of faith have little if any wakefulness about them.

Nevertheless, hope for heaven has its wakeful forms too. Carol Zaleski offers Christian reflections on near death experiences in a book entitled, *The Life of the World to Come.* Among the common themes in reports of those who claim to have returned from the other side, she offers the following:

> People who report near-death experiences insist that their state of awareness was not dreamlike but startlingly lucid—if anything, more real than life seems here below. It is as if they were given, within a dream, an intimation of what it would be like to be fully awake.[1]

Based on this observation, Zaleski proceeds with a discussion of how such experience satisfies the hope of wakeful Christians.

> What Christians hope for is not a pleasant dream but a complete awakening, compared to which our present existence will look like troubled sleep. What Christians hope for,

finally, is a collective awakening, an entry into a real world, compared to which our present world is almost fallen into nonbeing. And in that real world, Christians hope, every moment worth saving will be saved, every value eternally upheld, every species and person preserved.[2]

If wakeful Christians harbor a wish for heaven to fulfill, they wish not for an escape from reality, but for a deeper acquaintance with reality. When wakeful Christians lament this life, they grieve this world's trivialization of itself that obscures the more profound reality of the kingdom of God in our midst. Yet, more often wakeful Christians celebrate life, finding the mark of God's hand in this world and beginning their praise with the discovery of the holy here. "Holy, holy, holy is the LORD of hosts; / the whole earth is full of his glory" (Isaiah 6:3), the seraphim sang. Wakeful visions of otherworldly praise reveal angels singing of God's reign on earth as it is in heaven.

In chapter 2, we discussed how Jesus used his last meal with his disciples to teach them what the kingdom of God on earth looks like. I can only speculate about whether heaven looks something like that too. About the colors and contours, the orders and manners, the faces and places of heaven I can say nothing, having never visited there. We know little more about heaven except our hope for it and God's love for us, a love that relentlessly pursues us and infinitely longs to hold us, a love that conquered death before and promises to conquer it again.

With heaven shrouded in mystery, some escape this world into projections of how heaven will fulfill their wishes. Yet, for those who move beyond survival mode to higher wakefulness, the incarnation of God so closely weds this world and the next that death brings not an escape but a continuation, a deepening, an awakening. Death does not end our responsibility to heed God's call to draw near. We must be awake, ever obedient, ever seeking God's face before and beyond the last moment. Then we depart as if going though a door, anticipating a higher call to obedience and the clearer vision that comes with it.

WAKEFULNESS AND JUSTIFICATION

So what does it take in this life to enter the wakefulness of heaven in the next? Does it require not only faith but higher wakefulness? Will a simple faith that rarely if ever rises above survival mode suffice? Or does it require faith at all on this side of the grave?

I cannot begin to answer such questions adequately, but I cannot sidestep them either. Theological tomes on these questions undoubtedly gather dust on our library shelves, but the questions do not gather dust. These remain among the hottest questions on campus, so hot the religion faculty will seldom touch them. For two centuries, most intellectual elites of the west rested on the smug assumption that the larger culture would evolve to a point of indifference to questions about the afterlife. But just as death will not go away, so the questions remain.

Those questions too have a face, a face not as anguished, but pensive. She sought counseling for a decision about whether to take a semester off to relieve burnout. Her clear green eyes, wry sense of humor, and genuine love of learning delight her professors, none of whom seem to understand her desire to take time away for a breather. In an aside, she mentions her concern for a favorite professor whose outspoken skepticism about Christianity raised the ire of conservative Christian students. They confidently proclaim the professor's damnation for propagating such views without repentance. She asks, "How can God love us unconditionally but condemn us to hell if we don't say the password, 'Jesus Christ is my savior?'" In order to address that question and the others above it even in part, we must first review the theological idea of justification.

The words from Habakkuk cited earlier, "the righteous shall live by faith," had a profound impact on the apostle Paul. He used that phrase as the cornerstone of his doctrine of justification by faith (see Romans 1:17; Galatians 3:11). Justification means being right with God, having one's life lined up and on track with God's will. It entails the promise of a reward in the kingdom on earth or in heaven beyond.

In order to spread Christianity beyond Israel, Paul needed to push the point that God graciously justifies us through our faith. Other well-meaning Christians tried to introduce rites of initiation (e.g., circumcision) that seemed so strange to the Gentile converts that they served more as obstacles than means of grace. Moreover, Paul recognized that the idea of justification through our own actions creates the illusion that we achieve our own salvation when, in fact, God alone achieves our salvation through the death and resurrection of Christ.

In deference to Paul, I must submit that wakefulness does not justify us. Requiring wakefulness means sneaking in a new rite of passage to our justification, a rite of passage that makes justification seem our achievement rather than God's gift. Faith suffices, whether or not we enjoy its fruits through wakefulness. Faith without wakefulness is not faith without hope. Yet, faith without wakefulness misses the present day rewards of faith, and that is tragic indeed.

If we seek the kingdom in our rituals of rising and going to bed, in our work and leisure, in our family life and community life, we will know the rewards of faith before we die. If we seek God's face in the agnostic student hiding his eyes behind a baseball cap or the skeptical professor using class as a theological forum, the range of God's love will amaze us. If we focus on living our faith today and trusting God to take care of our neighbor's life after death, God will use our lives to reveal divine glory to our neighbor in God's time—in the next few moments or in a million years to come.

How do we reconcile the unconditional love of God with the condition that one must profess Jesus Christ as Lord to inherit heavenly bliss? That question reaches far beyond the scope of this book, but wakefulness addresses it indirectly by answering the conservative students who condemn the skeptical professor. Many will not come to faith under threat of torment after death, and for good reason. They take life on this earth too seriously to buy a faith that anxiously awaits another realm. One must show them the fruits of one's faith today, a difficult task when conducting an inquisition.

God's initiative alone justifies us, not our pious works, wakeful living, or saying the right creed. The skeptic's refusal to profess belief in Jesus Christ does not stop the loving work that Jesus Christ will do in and through the skeptic's life. The skeptic's brief years on this earth do not limit the time at Jesus' disposal to bring the skeptic fully justified to God.

Here is a final test of wakefulness: If after a lifetime of wakeful living we encounter in heaven the village atheist or Judas Iscariot or the preacher who slept around, will we rush to extend a welcome or shrink back in the shadows casting a suspicious glare? The wakeful will rush forward with joy.

Jesus told a parable about laborers in a vineyard who worked all day and complained that those who only worked an hour or two got the same wage. The landowner answered one of them:

> "Friend, I am doing you no wrong; did you not agree with me for the usual daily wage? Take what belongs to you and go; I choose to give to this last the same as I give to you. Am I not allowed to do what I choose with what belongs to me? Or are you envious because I am generous?" So the last will be first, and the first will be last.
>
> (Matthew 20:13-16)

God does not reward us because we labor long and well. God rewards us because God is generous.

Let us find satisfaction in wakefulness because it is God's bidding and the work is good, not because we proved ourselves or exceeded someone else. Let us rejoice at day's end over the abundance of God's gifts to us all.

QUESTIONS FOR REFLECTION AND DISCUSSION

1. Remember a time in your life or in the life of someone you know well when faith seemed especially rewarding despite troubles and pain. How did "the righteous live by faith" in that time?

2. Imagine that you are the counselor to one of the three young people who raise hard questions in this chapter. They include:

    a. The religious young woman who questioned the value of wakefulness for life on earth if the faithful still suffer in this life.

    b. The agnostic young man who questioned the motives of those who hope for heaven because he assumed that they only seek to escape responsibility for their life on earth.

    c. The bright young woman who wondered how a God of unconditional love could accept into heaven only those who profess that Jesus is Lord.

    Choose one and write a brief summary of how you would respond to them. Do not limit your answer to a rational argument. Address the emotional and spiritual needs the young person presents in posing the question. You may use your imagination to expand on the selected young questioner's personality and situation. If you are reading this as part of a group study, divide the group equally into three subgroups to address these young people and have each subgroup share their response with the whole group.

3. What idea or image in chapters 1–6 and 14 most challenged your outlook on your daily life with God? Write it down in one sentence. What idea or image in chapters 7–13 most challenged your behavior in your daily life with God? Write it down in one sentence. Compare the two statements. Pray for God to help you meet those challenges. If you read this book as part of a group study, let everyone share their challenges, and pray together for God to guide each person in facing them.

NOTES

CHAPTER 1

1. Abraham H. Maslow, *Motivation and Personality* (New York: Harper & Row, 1970), 35–47.
2. Charles R. Darwin, *On the Origin of Species by Means of Natural Selection, or The Preservation of Favoured Races in the Struggle for Life* (New York: Modern Library, 1993).

CHAPTER 3

1. The apocryphal book *The Acts of Paul and Thecla* describes Paul as a man "of a low stature, bald (or shaved) on the head, crooked thighs, handsome legs, hollow-eyed; had a crooked nose; full of grace; for sometimes he appeared as a man, sometimes he had the countenance of an angel" (1:7). See Rutherford H. Platt, Jr., Ed., *The Lost Books of the Bible* (Cleveland, Ohio: World Publishing; copyright 1926 by Alpha House), 100. Regarding Paul's speech quality, I take my cue from 2 Corinthians 10:10 and exercise a little poetic license.

CHAPTER 4

1. Bernhard W. Anderson, *Understanding the Old Testament*, 4th edition (Englewood Cliffs, N.J.: Prentice-Hall, 1986), 401. Also see Frank J. Matera, "Repentance," in *Harper's Bible Dictionary,* Paul J. Achtemeier, ed., (San Francisco: HarperCollins, 1985, 1996), 924.
2. Gerald G. May, *Addiction and Grace* (San Francisco: Harper & Row, 1988), 11.

CHAPTER 6

1. Abraham Joshua Heschel, *I Asked for Wonder: A Spiritual Anthology*, ed. Samuel H. Dresner (New York: Crossroad, 1992), 63.
2. For a classic discussion of this, see Erich Fromm, *Escape from Freedom*, (New York: Henry Holt, 1994).

CHAPTER 8

1. M. Robert Mulholland, Jr. *Shaped by the Word: The Power of Scripture in Spiritual Formation* (Nashville, Tenn.: Upper Room Books, 1985), 47–60.
2. Karl Barth, *The Word of God and the Word of Man* , trans. Douglas Horton (New York: Harper Torchbooks, 1957), 62–65. I must also call the readers attention to Frederick Buechner's rendering of Barth's parable in *Wishful Thinking: A Seeker's ABC* (San Francisco: HarperSanFrancisco, 1993), 9–10.
3. An excellent example of such a book is Reuben P. Job and Norman Shawchuck, *A Guide to Prayer* (Nashville, Tenn.: The Upper Room, 1983).

CHAPTER 9

1. Brother Lawrence of the Resurrection, *The Practice of the Presence of God* trans. John J. Delaney (New York: Image Books, 1997).

2. Viktor E. Frankl, *Man's Search for Meaning*, 3rd ed. (New York: Simon & Schuster, 1984).

3. Emil B. Berendt, "Work and Spirituality," *Spiritual Life*, 43, (Spring 1997): 49–52.

4. Robert N. Bellah, Richard Madsen, William M. Sullivan, Ann Swidler, and Stephen M. Tipton, *Habits of the Heart: Individualism and Commitment in American Life* (Berkeley, Calif.: University of California Press, 1985).

5. Frank Macchiarola, "Finding the Courage to Take Risks," in Gregory F. Augustine Pierce, ed., *Of Human Hands: A Reader in the Spirituality of Work* (Minneapolis, Minn.: Augsburg Fortress, 1991), 37–42.

6. John Scheible, "Called to Broaden My Horizon," in Pierce, *Of Human Hands*, 63–69.

7. Chris Satullo, "The Lord Catches Us in Our Craftiness," in Pierce, *Of Human Hands*, 91–96.

8. Maxine F. Dennis, "Compassion Is the Most Vital Tool of My Trade," in Pierce, *Of Human Hands*, 49–51.

9. Rose Mary Hart, "The Power and Presence of God Is Guiding My Way," in Pierce, *Of Human Hands*, 81–85.

10. Brother Lawrence, from "The Fourth Conversation," *Practice of the Presence*, p. 42.

11. Ibid., 102.

12. For this reading of Psalm 127:1-2, see the footnoted alternate translation from *The HarperCollins Study Bible: New Revised Standard Version* (New York: HarperCollins, 1993).

CHAPTER 10

1. Frederick Buechner, *Wishful Thinking: A Seeker's ABC*, rev. ed. (San Francisco: HarperSanFrancisco, 1993), 45.

2. Ibid.

3. Ibid., 46.

4. Ibid.

CHAPTER 11

1. Ernest Boyer, Jr., *Finding God at Home: Family Life as Spiritual Discipline* (San Francisco: HarperSanFrancisco, 1984), 3–5.

2. Ibid., 6–14.

3. Buechner, 119.

4. Paul Wilkes, "A Monk in the Bosom of His Family," in Pierce , *Of Human Hands,* 71.

5. Ibid.

6. Ibid.,70–76.

7. Marshall Jenkins, "Grandfather's Prayers," *The Christian Century* 110 (March 10, 1993): 260–261.

CHAPTER 12

1. Sharon Gallagher, "A Remembrance of Mother Teresa," *Radix* 25, no. 2: 20.

2. Ibid.

3. Ibid., 21.

4. Ibid.

5. Ibid.

6. Ibid., 20.

7. Reinhold Niebuhr, *The Nature and Destiny of Man*, 2 vols. (New York: Charles Scribner's Sons, 1941,1964).

8. For a spiritually provocative discussion of prophetic spirituality and political life, see Glenn Tinder, *The Political Meaning of Christianity: The Prophetic Stance* (San Francisco: HarperSanFrancisco, 1991).

CHAPTER 13

1. Abraham Joshua Heschel, *The Sabbath: Its Meaning for Modern Man*, (New York: Farrar, Straus, and Young, 1951) 3–10.

2. The reader who wishes to explore this topic further may read Morton T. Kelsey, *God, Dreams, and Revelation*, (Minneapolis, Minn.: Augsburg Fortress, 1991); Maria F. Mahoney, *The Meaning of Dreams and Dreaming*, (Secaucus, N.J.: Citadel Press, 1966); John A. Sanford, *Dreams: God's Forgotten Language* (Philadelphia, Pa.: J.B. Lippincott Company, 1968).

CHAPTER 14

1. Carol Zaleski, *The Life of the World to Come: Near Death Experience and Christian Hope*, (New York: Oxford University Press 1996), 67.

2. Ibid.

About the Author

J. Marshall Jenkins is Director of Counseling at Berry College and a psychologist in private practice in Rome, Georgia. He is a member of several organizations including the Amerian Psychological Association and the American Assocation of Pastoral Counselors. The author has also taught counseling, psychology, and religion courses at various colleges and has led numerous worskhops.

Jenkins received his Ph.D. in Counseling Psychology from the University of North Carolina at Chapel Hill in 1986 and his B.A. in Philosophy from Davidson College in 1980. He is the author of *The Ancient Laugh of God: Divine Encounters in Unlikely Places*, and he has published articles in *The Christian Century*, *Lectionary Homiletics*, and *The Pastoral Forum*. He and his wife, Sharon, are the proud parents of a young son, Philip.